Anti Inflammatory Diet Cookbook For Beginners

Transform Your Diet with Nutritious and Delicious Recipes to Strengthen Your Immune System and Achieve Total Wellness

Franz Geissler

© Copyright 2024 by Franz Geissler - All rights reserved.

This document is geared towards providing exact and reliable information in regard to the topic and issue covered.

- From a Declaration of Principles which was accepted and approved equally by a Committee of the American Bar Association and a Committee of Publishers and Associations.

In no way is it legal to reproduce, duplicate, or transmit any part of this document in either electronic means or in printed format. All rights reserved.

The information provided herein is stated to be truthful and consistent, in that any liability, in terms of inattention or otherwise, by any usage or abuse of any policies, processes, or directions contained within is the solitary and utter responsibility of the recipient reader. Under no circumstances will any legal responsibility or blame be held against the publisher for any reparation, damages, or monetary loss due to the information herein, either directly or indirectly.

Respective authors own all copyrights not held by the publisher.

The information herein is offered for informational purposes solely and is universal as so. The presentation of the information is without contract or any type of guarantee assurance.

The trademarks that are used are without any consent, and the publication of the trademark is without permission or backing by the trademark owner. All trademarks and brands within this book are for clarifying purposes only and are owned by the owners themselves, not affiliated with this document.

Access the bonus

Scroll to the end and scan the QR code

Table Of Contents

INTRODUCTION 4

CHAPTER 1: UNDERSTANDING THE ANTI-INFLAMMATORY DIET 5
- What is an Anti-inflammatory Diet? 5
- Benefits of an Anti-inflammatory Diet 6
- Scientific Foundations 8

CHAPTER 2: GETTING STARTED 10
- Stocking Your Pantry: Essential Ingredients 10
- Tips and Tricks for Beginners 11

CHAPTER 3: BREAKFAST IDEAS 13
- Nutrient-Rich Smoothies 13
- Healthy Breakfast Bowls 21

CHAPTER 4: LUNCH OPTIONS 30
- Simple and Quick Salads 30
- Satisfying Soups and Stews 39

CHAPTER 5: DINNER RECIPES 48
- Light and Delicious Dinner Dishes 48
- Fish and Seafood for Beginners 61

CHAPTER 6: SNACKS AND SMALL MEALS 73
- Healthy Snacks for In-Between 73
- Anti-inflammatory Desserts 84

CHAPTER 7: 28-DAY MEAL PLAN 97
- Shopping List 100

CHAPTER 9: FREQUENTLY ASKED QUESTIONS 102
- Myths and Facts about the Anti-inflammatory Diet 102
- Common Mistakes and How to Avoid Them 103

CONCLUSION 105

Introduction

Welcome to a new journey toward optimal health and wellness. This book is designed for anyone who wants to improve their diet, reduce inflammation in their body, and strengthen their immune system through balanced nutrition and delicious recipes. Are you a busy professional with little time for complex meal preparation? Don't worry, you're in the right place. Simplicity and practicality are at the heart of our recipes and tips.

Chronic inflammation is an increasing problem in modern society, often linked to diets high in processed foods, refined sugars, and saturated fats. These factors can contribute to a range of health issues, including heart disease, diabetes, arthritis, and many other chronic conditions. However, you can counteract these negative effects by adopting a more natural and nutritious diet.

In this book, we will explore how an anti-inflammatory diet can become a fundamental part of your daily routine, even if you have a busy schedule. You will learn how to choose the right ingredients, plan meals in advance, and prepare dishes that are not only good for you but also delicious. You'll find a variety of recipes suitable for every meal of the day, along with snacks and desserts that will help you stay on track toward better health without sacrificing flavor.

Our goal is to provide you with practical tools and science-based knowledge to help you make better dietary choices. With a bit of planning and commitment, you will discover that following an anti-inflammatory diet is possible even with a hectic lifestyle. Soon, you'll realize that eating healthy is not only achievable but also enjoyable.

Chapter 1: Understanding the Anti-inflammatory Diet

What is an Anti-inflammatory Diet?

An anti-inflammatory diet is more than just a meal plan; it's a holistic approach to eating that prioritizes foods known to combat chronic inflammation in the body. Inflammation is the body's natural response to injury or illness, an essential part of the healing process. However, when this response becomes chronic, it can lead to various health issues, including arthritis, cardiovascular disease, and even some forms of cancer.

This nutritional strategy is rooted in consuming a variety of nutrient-rich foods that naturally reduce inflammation. These include fruits, vegetables, whole grains, lean proteins, and healthy fats. The focus is on eating foods in their most natural state, minimizing processed items and those high in added sugars and unhealthy fats.

Imagine starting your day with a breakfast bowl filled with fresh berries, chia seeds, and a sprinkle of nuts, all drizzled with a touch of honey. Each ingredient in this simple meal contributes to reducing inflammation. Berries are packed with antioxidants, which help neutralize free radicals that can cause cellular damage. Chia seeds are rich in omega-3 fatty acids, known for their anti-inflammatory properties. Nuts provide a healthy dose of essential fats and vitamins.

Lunch might be a colorful salad with leafy greens, tomatoes, cucumbers, and avocados, topped with grilled salmon. Leafy greens, like spinach and kale, are high in vitamins and minerals that support the body's healing processes. Tomatoes contain lycopene, an antioxidant that helps combat inflammation. Avocados are rich in monounsaturated fats, which have been shown to reduce inflammatory markers in the body. Salmon, a fatty fish, is an excellent source of omega-3 fatty acids. For dinner, consider a hearty quinoa bowl with roasted vegetables and a side of steamed broccoli. Quinoa, a whole grain, is a complete protein, providing all the essential amino acids needed for body repair and maintenance. Roasted vegetables, such as sweet potatoes, carrots, and bell peppers, are packed with vitamins and fiber, supporting digestive health and reducing inflammation. Broccoli, a cruciferous vegetable, contains sulforaphane, a compound that helps reduce inflammation and may protect against chronic diseases.

This approach to eating is not just about what you consume but also about what you avoid. Reducing the intake of processed foods, refined carbohydrates, and excessive amounts of red and processed meats is crucial. These foods can contribute to inflammation, exacerbating health issues.

Benefits of an Anti-inflammatory Diet

One of the primary advantages of following this nutritional regimen is the significant reduction in the risk of chronic diseases. Consuming foods that fight inflammation can help protect against heart disease, diabetes, and certain cancers. For example, antioxidants found in fruits and vegetables neutralize harmful free radicals, thereby reducing oxidative stress, a key contributor to chronic illness.

Another compelling benefit is the improvement in joint health. Inflammatory conditions like arthritis can cause debilitating pain and stiffness. By incorporating foods that have natural anti-inflammatory properties, such as omega-3-rich fish or antioxidant-packed berries, you can alleviate these symptoms and improve mobility. Many people who adopt this way of eating report less pain and greater ease of movement.

Weight management is also a significant perk. Chronic inflammation is often linked to weight gain and difficulty losing weight. By reducing inflammation, this diet helps to normalize metabolic processes and can aid in achieving and maintaining a healthy weight. Whole foods like fruits, vegetables, and whole grains are nutrient-dense and low in calories, making it easier to control your weight without feeling deprived.

The positive effects extend to your mental health as well. There is growing evidence that inflammation can affect brain function and mood. Nutrient-rich foods that reduce inflammation can also enhance brain health, potentially lowering the risk of depression and cognitive decline. Omega-3 fatty acids, for example, are known to support brain function and are found abundantly in fatty fish, flaxseeds, and walnuts.

Additionally, digestive health sees marked improvements. A diet high in fiber from fruits, vegetables, and whole grains supports a healthy gut microbiome. A balanced gut can reduce inflammation and improve overall digestive function, reducing symptoms of bloating, constipation, and irritable bowel syndrome.

Skin health benefits are also noteworthy. Chronic inflammation can manifest as skin issues like acne, psoriasis, and eczema. An eating pattern that includes anti-inflammatory foods can lead to clearer, healthier skin. Foods rich in vitamins and antioxidants, such as leafy greens and nuts, provide the nutrients necessary for skin repair and regeneration.

Furthermore, this dietary approach promotes overall longevity. By mitigating chronic inflammation, you support your body's ability to repair itself and resist age-related diseases. Many centenarians around the world follow a diet naturally high in anti-inflammatory foods, contributing to their long and healthy lives.

Scientific Foundations

The principles behind an anti-inflammatory diet are supported by a robust body of scientific research, which highlights the profound impact of diet on inflammation and overall health. Understanding these scientific foundations can empower you to make informed choices that benefit your long-term well-being.

At the core of this nutritional approach is the concept of inflammation itself. Inflammation is a biological response to harmful stimuli, such as pathogens, damaged cells, or irritants. It is a crucial part of the body's immune response, aimed at eliminating the initial cause of cell injury, clearing out necrotic cells and tissues, and establishing tissue repair. However, when inflammation becomes chronic, it can lead to a host of health problems, including cardiovascular disease, diabetes, cancer, and neurodegenerative conditions.

Scientific studies have consistently shown that certain foods and dietary patterns can either promote or reduce chronic inflammation. For example, diets high in processed foods, trans fats, and refined sugars are linked to increased inflammatory markers in the body. These dietary components can activate inflammatory pathways, leading to elevated levels of C-reactive protein (CRP) and other inflammatory markers.

Conversely, diets rich in fruits, vegetables, whole grains, and healthy fats are associated with lower levels of inflammation. These foods are abundant in antioxidants, which help neutralize free radicals and reduce oxidative stress. Antioxidants like vitamins C and E, polyphenols, and carotenoids are found in colorful fruits and vegetables and play a crucial role in mitigating inflammation.

Omega-3 fatty acids, found in fatty fish, flaxseeds, and walnuts, are another cornerstone of this dietary approach. These essential fats have been shown to inhibit the production of inflammatory cytokines and eicosanoids, which are molecules involved in the inflammatory response. Numerous studies have demonstrated that increasing omega-3 intake can significantly reduce inflammation and improve outcomes in conditions such as rheumatoid arthritis, cardiovascular disease, and depression.

Moreover, the role of the gut microbiome in inflammation is a burgeoning area of research. The gut microbiome consists of trillions of microorganisms that live in our digestive tract and have a profound impact on our health. A diet high in fiber from fruits, vegetables, and whole grains supports a diverse and healthy microbiome. These beneficial bacteria produce short-chain fatty acids (SCFAs) during the fermentation of dietary fiber, which have anti-inflammatory properties and help maintain the integrity of the gut barrier. Disruptions in the gut microbiome, often caused by a poor diet, can lead to increased intestinal permeability, or "leaky gut," which allows inflammatory compounds to enter the bloodstream and trigger systemic inflammation.

Furthermore, phytochemicals, naturally occurring compounds found in plants, also contribute to the anti-inflammatory effects of this diet. Compounds such as flavonoids, found in berries and green tea, and curcumin, found in turmeric, have been extensively studied for their ability to modulate inflammatory pathways. These compounds can inhibit the activity of nuclear factor kappa B (NF-κB), a protein complex that plays a pivotal role in regulating the immune response to infection and inflammation.

The scientific basis for this dietary approach is also supported by epidemiological studies that examine dietary patterns and health outcomes in large populations. For example, the Mediterranean diet, which shares many principles with the anti-inflammatory diet, has been associated with reduced inflammatory markers and a lower risk of chronic diseases. Populations that adhere to this diet tend to have lower rates of cardiovascular disease, cancer, and cognitive decline, suggesting a protective effect against inflammation-related conditions.

Chapter 2: Getting Started

Stocking Your Pantry: Essential Ingredients

First, let's talk about the power of whole grains. Whole grains such as quinoa, brown rice, and oats are fantastic staples. These grains are packed with fiber, vitamins, and minerals, which are known to reduce inflammation and promote digestive health. Quinoa, for instance, is a complete protein, providing all nine essential amino acids your body needs. Brown rice offers a hearty base for many dishes, while oats are perfect for a nourishing breakfast or baking.

Next, it's essential to include a variety of legumes in your pantry. Beans, lentils, and chickpeas are not only affordable but also versatile. They are rich in fiber and plant-based protein, helping to stabilize blood sugar levels and keep inflammation at bay. Imagine a comforting lentil soup simmering on the stove or a vibrant chickpea salad tossed with fresh vegetables and herbs. These legumes provide a solid nutritional foundation for numerous meals.

Healthy fats are another cornerstone of an anti-inflammatory kitchen. Olive oil, avocado oil, and coconut oil are excellent choices. Olive oil, in particular, is renowned for its anti-inflammatory properties due to its high content of monounsaturated fats and antioxidants. Avocado oil is perfect for high-heat cooking, and coconut oil adds a delightful richness to various dishes. Nuts and seeds, such as almonds, walnuts, chia seeds, and flaxseeds, are also must-haves. They provide omega-3 fatty acids, protein, and fiber, all of which contribute to reducing inflammation and supporting heart health.

Your pantry should also boast a robust selection of herbs and spices. Turmeric, ginger, garlic, cinnamon, and cayenne pepper are not only flavorful but also packed with anti-inflammatory compounds. Turmeric, for example, contains curcumin, a powerful anti-inflammatory agent. Adding these spices to your meals can enhance flavor and provide numerous health benefits. Think of a golden turmeric latte to start your day or a spicy ginger stir-fry for dinner.

Canned or jarred goods, such as tomatoes, olives, and artichokes, can be lifesavers for quick and healthy meals. Tomatoes, especially when cooked, are high in lycopene, an antioxidant that fights inflammation. Olives and artichokes add depth and nutrition to salads and pastas, making them excellent pantry staples.

Don't forget about your sweeteners. While it's essential to minimize refined sugars, natural sweeteners like honey, maple syrup, and dates can be used in moderation. These sweeteners offer a more wholesome alternative and can be used in baking or to sweeten your morning oatmeal.

Tips and Tricks for Beginners

Starting a new dietary regimen can feel overwhelming, but with a few practical tips and tricks, you can transition smoothly and enjoy the journey toward better health. Here are some strategies to help you get started and stay on track.

First, take it one step at a time. It's important not to overhaul your entire diet overnight. Begin by making small, manageable changes. For instance, swap out refined grains for whole grains, like replacing white rice with quinoa or brown rice. Gradually introduce more fruits and vegetables into your meals. This gradual approach helps you adjust without feeling deprived or overwhelmed.

Meal planning and preparation are key to success. Spend some time each week planning your meals and snacks. Having a plan reduces the temptation to reach for unhealthy options when you're hungry and pressed for time. Consider preparing meals in batches. Cook a large pot of quinoa or brown rice and roast a variety of vegetables at the beginning of the week. These can be mixed and matched to create different meals throughout the week, saving you time and effort.

Another effective strategy is to keep healthy snacks readily available. Stock your pantry and fridge with nuts, seeds, fresh fruits, and cut-up vegetables. These snacks are not only nutritious but also easy to grab when you're on the go. Preparing snack-sized portions in advance can make healthy eating convenient and stress-free.

Learning to read food labels can also make a big difference. Pay attention to the ingredients list and nutritional information on packaged foods. Look out for hidden sugars, unhealthy fats, and artificial additives. Aim to choose products with minimal ingredients and those that are as close to their natural state as possible. This helps ensure you're consuming foods that support your health rather than hinder it.

Spice up your meals with herbs and spices. These not only add flavor but also offer various health benefits. Experiment with different combinations to keep your meals interesting and flavorful. For example, adding turmeric to your scrambled eggs or cinnamon to your morning oatmeal can provide a nutritional boost while enhancing taste.

Staying hydrated is another crucial aspect. Often, feelings of hunger can actually be signs of dehydration. Drink plenty of water throughout the day. Herbal teas and infused water with slices of citrus fruits or cucumber can also be refreshing and hydrating options.

Don't forget to listen to your body. Everyone's needs are different, so pay attention to how different foods make you feel. Some foods might cause discomfort or bloating, while others might make you feel energized and satisfied. Keeping a food diary can help you track these reactions and make adjustments to your diet accordingly.

Chapter 3: Breakfast Ideas

Nutrient-Rich Smoothies

1. Green Power Smoothie

Preparation Time: 10 minutes | **Serving Size:** 2

Ingredients:
- 2 cups spinach leaves
- 1 banana
- 1 apple, cored and chopped
- 1/2 avocado
- 1 cup unsweetened almond milk
- 1 tablespoon chia seeds
- 1 teaspoon spirulina powder (optional)
- Ice cubes as needed

Mode of cooking:
- Blending

Procedure:
1. Rinse the spinach leaves thoroughly under cold water.
2. Peel and slice the banana, then core and chop the apple.
3. Scoop out the flesh of the avocado.
4. Combine all ingredients, including the spinach, banana, apple, avocado, almond milk, chia seeds, and spirulina powder, in a blender.
5. Blend on high until smooth and creamy, adding ice cubes if desired for a colder smoothie.

Nutrition (Per serving): Calories: 230 | Fat: 10g | Carbs: 30g | Protein: 5g | Sugar: 14g | Sodium: 60mg

2. Berry Bliss Smoothie

Preparation Time: 10 minutes | **Serving Size:** 2

Ingredients:
- 1 cup mixed berries (strawberries, blueberries, raspberries)
- 1 banana
- 1/2 cup Greek yogurt
- 1 cup coconut water
- 1 tablespoon flaxseeds
- 1 tablespoon honey (optional)
- Ice cubes as needed

Mode of cooking:
- Blending

Procedure:
1. Rinse the mixed berries and peel the banana.
2. Slice the banana and measure out the Greek yogurt and coconut water.
3. Add the berries, banana, Greek yogurt, coconut water, and flaxseeds to a blender.
4. Blend until smooth, adding honey for sweetness if desired.
5. Adjust the thickness with ice cubes and blend again until fully combined.

Nutrition (Per serving): Calories: 200 | Fat: 4g | Carbs: 35g | Protein: 7g | Sugar: 20g | Sodium: 70mg

3. Tropical Delight Smoothie

Preparation Time: 10 minutes | **Serving Size:** 2

Ingredients:
- 1 cup pineapple chunks
- 1 cup mango chunks
- 1 banana
- 1 cup coconut milk
- 1 tablespoon hemp seeds
- 1 teaspoon turmeric powder
- Ice cubes as needed

Mode of cooking:
- Blending

Procedure:
1. Prepare the pineapple and mango chunks, and peel and slice the banana.
2. Measure out the coconut milk and gather the hemp seeds and turmeric powder.
3. Place all ingredients, including the pineapple, mango, banana, coconut milk, hemp seeds, and turmeric, into a blender.
4. Blend until smooth, adding ice cubes for a thicker consistency if desired.
5. Serve immediately, ensuring a creamy and well-mixed texture.

Nutrition (Per serving): Calories: 250 | Fat: 8g | Carbs: 42g | Protein: 4g | Sugar: 30g | Sodium: 45mg

4. Almond Berry Smoothie

Preparation Time: 10 minutes | **Serving Size:** 2

Ingredients:
- 1 cup almond milk
- 1 cup mixed berries (blackberries, blueberries, strawberries)
- 1 tablespoon almond butter
- 1 banana
- 1 tablespoon chia seeds

- 1 teaspoon vanilla extract
- Ice cubes as needed

Mode of cooking:
- Blending

Procedure:
1. Rinse the mixed berries and peel the banana.
2. Slice the banana and measure out the almond milk, almond butter, and chia seeds.
3. Combine all ingredients in a blender, including the almond milk, berries, almond butter, banana, chia seeds, and vanilla extract.
4. Blend on high until smooth and creamy, adding ice cubes for a thicker smoothie if desired.
5. Pour into glasses and serve immediately.

Nutrition (Per serving): Calories: 210 | Fat: 10g | Carbs: 28g | Protein: 5g | Sugar: 14g | Sodium: 80mg

5. Matcha Green Tea Smoothie

Preparation Time: 10 minutes | **Serving Size:** 2

Ingredients:
- 1 banana
- 1 cup baby spinach
- 1/2 avocado
- 1 cup unsweetened almond milk
- 1 teaspoon matcha green tea powder
- 1 tablespoon honey (optional)
- Ice cubes as needed

Mode of cooking:
- Blending

Procedure:
1. Peel and slice the banana, and prepare the baby spinach.
2. Scoop out the avocado flesh and measure the almond milk and matcha powder.
3. Add all ingredients, including the banana, spinach, avocado, almond milk, matcha powder, and honey (if using), to a blender.
4. Blend until smooth, adding ice cubes to achieve desired consistency.

5. Serve chilled and enjoy the refreshing taste.

Nutrition (Per serving): Calories: 220 | Fat: 11g | Carbs: 29g | Protein: 4g | Sugar: 13g | Sodium: 70mg

6. Chocolate Banana Smoothie

Preparation Time: 10 minutes | **Serving Size:** 2

Ingredients:
- 2 bananas
- 2 tablespoons cocoa powder
- 1 cup unsweetened almond milk
- 1 tablespoon flaxseeds
- 1 tablespoon honey (optional)
- 1/2 teaspoon cinnamon
- Ice cubes as needed

Mode of cooking:
- Blending

Procedure:
1. Peel and slice the bananas.
2. Measure out the cocoa powder, almond milk, flaxseeds, and honey.
3. Place the bananas, cocoa powder, almond milk, flaxseeds, honey, and cinnamon into a blender.
4. Blend on high until smooth and creamy, adding ice cubes for a thicker consistency if desired.
5. Pour into glasses and serve immediately for a rich and nutritious treat.

Nutrition (Per serving): Calories: 240 | Fat: 7g | Carbs: 43g | Protein: 5g | Sugar: 22g | Sodium: 60mg

7. Pumpkin Spice Smoothie

Preparation Time: 10 minutes | **Serving Size:** 2

Ingredients:
- 1 cup pumpkin puree
- 1 banana
- 1 cup unsweetened almond milk
- 1 tablespoon chia seeds
- 1 teaspoon pumpkin spice blend
- 1 tablespoon maple syrup (optional)
- Ice cubes as needed

Mode of cooking:
- Blending

Procedure:
1. Peel and slice the banana.
2. Measure out the pumpkin puree, almond milk, chia seeds, and pumpkin spice blend.
3. Combine all ingredients in a blender, including the banana, pumpkin puree, almond milk, chia seeds, pumpkin spice blend, and maple syrup (if using).
4. Blend until smooth, adding ice cubes for a thicker consistency if desired.
5. Serve chilled and enjoy the seasonal flavors.

Nutrition (Per serving): Calories: 210 | Fat: 6g | Carbs: 38g | Protein: 4g | Sugar: 18g | Sodium: 65mg

8. Blueberry Oat Smoothie

Preparation Time: 10 minutes | **Serving Size:** 2

Ingredients:
- 1 cup blueberries
- 1/2 cup rolled oats
- 1 banana
- 1 cup unsweetened almond milk
- 1 tablespoon hemp seeds
- 1 teaspoon vanilla extract

- Ice cubes as needed

Mode of cooking:
- Blending

Procedure:
1. Rinse the blueberries and peel the banana.
2. Measure out the rolled oats, almond milk, and hemp seeds.
3. Add all ingredients, including the blueberries, oats, banana, almond milk, hemp seeds, and vanilla extract, to a blender.
4. Blend on high until smooth and creamy, adding ice cubes for desired thickness.
5. Serve immediately and enjoy the hearty and nutritious blend.

Nutrition (Per serving): Calories: 250 | Fat: 7g | Carbs: 42g | Protein: 6g | Sugar: 16g | Sodium: 55mg

9. Avocado Pineapple Smoothie

Preparation Time: 10 minutes | **Serving Size:** 2

Ingredients:
- 1/2 avocado
- 1 cup pineapple chunks
- 1 banana
- 1 cup coconut water
- 1 tablespoon chia seeds
- 1 teaspoon lime juice
- Ice cubes as needed

Mode of cooking:
- Blending

Procedure:
1. Scoop out the avocado flesh and peel and slice the banana.
2. Measure out the pineapple chunks and coconut water.
3. Place the avocado, pineapple, banana, coconut water, chia seeds, and lime juice into a blender.
4. Blend on high until smooth, adding ice cubes to achieve desired consistency.
5. Serve chilled for a refreshing tropical treat.

Nutrition (Per serving): Calories: 220 | Fat: 9g | Carbs: 35g | Protein: 3g | Sugar: 20g | Sodium: 40mg

10. Spinach Pear Smoothie

Preparation Time: 10 minutes | **Serving Size:** 2

Ingredients:
- 2 cups baby spinach
- 1 pear, cored and chopped
- 1 banana
- 1 cup unsweetened almond milk
- 1 tablespoon flaxseeds
- 1 teaspoon honey (optional)
- Ice cubes as needed

Mode of cooking:
- Blending

Procedure:
1. Rinse the spinach and peel and slice the banana.
2. Core and chop the pear.
3. Measure out the almond milk and flaxseeds.
4. Combine all ingredients in a blender, including the spinach, pear, banana, almond milk, flaxseeds, and honey (if using).
5. Blend on high until smooth, adding ice cubes to achieve desired consistency.
6. Pour into glasses and serve immediately.

Nutrition (Per serving): Calories: 210 | Fat: 5g | Carbs: 38g | Protein: 4g | Sugar: 18g | Sodium: 50mg

Healthy Breakfast Bowls

11. Quinoa Fruit Bowl

Preparation Time: 10 minutes | **Cooking Time:** 15 minutes | **Serving Size:** 2

Ingredients:
- 1 cup quinoa
- 2 cups water
- 1 banana, sliced
- 1 cup mixed berries (strawberries, blueberries, raspberries)
- 2 tablespoons almond butter
- 1 tablespoon chia seeds
- 1 teaspoon honey (optional)

Mode of cooking:
- Boiling and assembling

Procedure:
1. Rinse the quinoa under cold water to remove any bitterness.
2. In a medium saucepan, bring the water to a boil. Add the quinoa, reduce the heat, and simmer for 15 minutes or until the water is absorbed.
3. While the quinoa is cooking, slice the banana and prepare the mixed berries.
4. Once the quinoa is cooked, fluff it with a fork and divide it into two bowls.
5. Top each bowl with banana slices, mixed berries, a dollop of almond butter, and a sprinkle of chia seeds. Drizzle with honey if desired.

Nutrition (Per serving): Calories: 350 | Fat: 12g | Carbs: 55g | Protein: 10g | Sugar: 15g | Sodium: 10mg

12. Almond Joy Smoothie Bowl

Preparation Time: 10 minutes | **Cooking Time:** 0 minutes | **Serving Size:** 2

Ingredients:
- 1 banana, frozen
- 1 cup unsweetened almond milk
- 2 tablespoons almond butter
- 2 tablespoons cocoa powder
- 1 tablespoon chia seeds
- 1/4 cup granola
- 2 tablespoons shredded coconut
- 1 tablespoon dark chocolate chips

Mode of cooking:
- Blending and assembling

Procedure:
1. Peel and slice the frozen banana.
2. In a blender, combine the banana, almond milk, almond butter, cocoa powder, and chia seeds. Blend until smooth and thick.
3. Pour the smoothie into two bowls.
4. Top each bowl with granola, shredded coconut, and dark chocolate chips.
5. Serve immediately for a creamy, indulgent breakfast.

Nutrition (Per serving): Calories: 320 | Fat: 16g | Carbs: 40g | Protein: 8g | Sugar: 20g | Sodium: 60mg

13. Chia Pudding Bowl

Preparation Time: 10 minutes | **Cooking Time:** 0 minutes (overnight refrigeration) | **Serving Size:** 2

Ingredients:
- 1/2 cup chia seeds
- 2 cups unsweetened almond milk
- 1 teaspoon vanilla extract
- 1 tablespoon maple syrup
- 1 cup sliced strawberries
- 1/4 cup pumpkin seeds
- 1 kiwi, sliced

Mode of cooking:
- Mixing and refrigeration

Procedure:
1. In a medium bowl, combine chia seeds, almond milk, vanilla extract, and maple syrup. Stir well to prevent clumping.
2. Cover the bowl and refrigerate overnight or for at least 4 hours until the mixture thickens.
3. Once the chia pudding is set, give it a good stir and divide it into two bowls.
4. Top each bowl with sliced strawberries, pumpkin seeds, and kiwi slices.
5. Serve chilled for a refreshing and nutritious breakfast.

Nutrition (Per serving): Calories: 280 | Fat: 12g | Carbs: 35g | Protein: 10g | Sugar: 14g | Sodium: 45mg

14. Tropical Overnight Oats

Preparation Time: 10 minutes | **Cooking Time:** 0 minutes (overnight refrigeration) | **Serving Size:** 2

Ingredients:
- 1 cup rolled oats
- 1 cup coconut milk
- 1/2 cup Greek yogurt
- 1 tablespoon honey
- 1/2 mango, diced
- 1/2 pineapple, diced
- 1 tablespoon chia seeds

Mode of cooking:
- Mixing and refrigeration

Procedure:
1. In a medium bowl, combine rolled oats, coconut milk, Greek yogurt, and honey. Stir well.
2. Cover the bowl and refrigerate overnight or for at least 4 hours until the oats are soft.
3. In the morning, give the oats a good stir and divide into two bowls.
4. Top each bowl with diced mango, pineapple, and a sprinkle of chia seeds.
5. Serve cold and enjoy a taste of the tropics.

Nutrition (Per serving): Calories: 320 | Fat: 12g | Carbs: 50g | Protein: 10g | Sugar: 20g | Sodium: 60mg

15. Savory Avocado Quinoa Bowl

Preparation Time: 10 minutes | **Cooking Time:** 15 minutes | **Serving Size:** 2

Ingredients:
- 1 cup quinoa
- 2 cups water
- 1 avocado, sliced
- 1/2 cup cherry tomatoes, halved
- 1/4 cup red onion, diced
- 2 tablespoons pumpkin seeds
- 1 tablespoon olive oil
- 1 tablespoon lemon juice
- Salt and pepper to taste

Mode of cooking:
- Boiling and assembling

Procedure:
1. Rinse the quinoa under cold water.
2. In a medium saucepan, bring the water to a boil. Add the quinoa, reduce the heat, and simmer for 15 minutes or until the water is absorbed.
3. While the quinoa is cooking, slice the avocado and halve the cherry tomatoes.
4. Once the quinoa is cooked, fluff with a fork and divide into two bowls.
5. Top each bowl with avocado slices, cherry tomatoes, red onion, and pumpkin seeds. Drizzle with olive oil and lemon juice. Season with salt and pepper.

Nutrition (Per serving): Calories: 350 | Fat: 18g | Carbs: 40g | Protein: 10g | Sugar: 5g | Sodium: 70mg

16. Blueberry Almond Breakfast Bowl

Preparation Time: 10 minutes | **Cooking Time:** 0 minutes | **Serving Size:** 2

Ingredients:
- 1 cup Greek yogurt
- 1/2 cup rolled oats
- 1 cup blueberries
- 2 tablespoons almond butter
- 2 tablespoons slivered almonds
- 1 tablespoon honey

Mode of cooking:
- Assembling

Procedure:
1. Measure out the Greek yogurt and rolled oats.
2. In two bowls, divide the Greek yogurt evenly.
3. Top each bowl with rolled oats, blueberries, a dollop of almond butter, and slivered almonds.
4. Drizzle with honey.
5. Serve immediately for a nutritious and satisfying breakfast.

Nutrition (Per serving): Calories: 300 | Fat: 12g | Carbs: 35g | Protein: 15g | Sugar: 15g | Sodium: 55mg

17. Apple Cinnamon Breakfast Bowl

Preparation Time: 10 minutes | **Cooking Time:** 5 minutes | **Serving Size:** 2

Ingredients:
- 1 cup rolled oats
- 2 cups water
- 1 apple, diced
- 1 tablespoon chia seeds
- 1 teaspoon cinnamon
- 1 tablespoon maple syrup
- 1/4 cup walnuts, chopped

Mode of cooking:
- Boiling and assembling

Procedure:
1. In a medium saucepan, bring the water to a boil.
2. Add the rolled oats, reduce the heat, and simmer for 5 minutes or until the oats are cooked.
3. While the oats are cooking, dice the apple.
4. Divide the cooked oats into two bowls.
5. Top each bowl with diced apple, chia seeds, cinnamon, maple syrup, and chopped walnuts. Serve warm.

Nutrition (Per serving): Calories: 310 | Fat: 10g | Carbs: 50g | Protein: 8g | Sugar: 15g | Sodium: 10mg

18.   Banana Nut Breakfast Bowl

Preparation Time: 10 minutes | **Cooking Time:** 0 minutes | **Serving Size:** 2

Ingredients:
- 2 bananas, sliced
- 1 cup Greek yogurt
- 1/2 cup granola
- 2 tablespoons almond butter
- 2 tablespoons flaxseeds
- 1 tablespoon honey (optional)

Mode of cooking:
- Assembling

Procedure:
1. Peel and slice the bananas.
2. Divide the Greek yogurt evenly into two bowls.
3. Top each bowl with sliced bananas, granola, a dollop of almond butter, and flaxseeds.
4. Drizzle with honey if desired.
5. Serve immediately for a nutritious and satisfying breakfast.

Nutrition (Per serving): Calories: 350 | Fat: 15g | Carbs: 45g | Protein: 12g | Sugar: 20g | Sodium: 60mg

19. Tropical Chia Bowl

Preparation Time: 10 minutes | **Cooking Time:** 0 minutes (overnight refrigeration) | **Serving Size:** 2

Ingredients:
- 1/2 cup chia seeds
- 2 cups coconut milk
- 1 teaspoon vanilla extract
- 1/2 cup diced mango
- 1/2 cup diced pineapple
- 1/4 cup shredded coconut
- 1 tablespoon honey (optional)

Mode of cooking:
- Mixing and refrigeration

Procedure:
1. In a medium bowl, combine chia seeds, coconut milk, and vanilla extract. Stir well to prevent clumping.
2. Cover the bowl and refrigerate overnight or for at least 4 hours until the mixture thickens.
3. Once the chia pudding is set, give it a good stir and divide it into two bowls.
4. Top each bowl with diced mango, pineapple, and shredded coconut. Drizzle with honey if desired.
5. Serve chilled for a refreshing and nutritious breakfast.

Nutrition (Per serving): Calories: 320 | Fat: 20g | Carbs: 30g | Protein: 6g | Sugar: 15g | Sodium: 50mg

20. Sweet Potato Breakfast Bowl

Preparation Time: 10 minutes | **Cooking Time:** 20 minutes | **Serving Size:** 2

Ingredients:
- 1 large sweet potato, peeled and cubed
- 1/2 cup Greek yogurt
- 1 tablespoon almond butter
- 1 tablespoon honey
- 1/4 cup pecans, chopped
- 1/2 teaspoon cinnamon

Mode of cooking:
- Boiling and assembling

Procedure:
1. In a medium saucepan, bring water to a boil. Add the sweet potato cubes and cook for 20 minutes or until tender.
2. Drain the sweet potatoes and mash them with a fork.
3. Divide the mashed sweet potatoes into two bowls.
4. Top each bowl with Greek yogurt, almond butter, honey, chopped pecans, and a sprinkle of cinnamon.
5. Serve warm for a comforting and nutritious breakfast.

Nutrition (Per serving): Calories: 330 | Fat: 12g | Carbs: 45g | Protein: 8g | Sugar: 20g | Sodium: 30mg

Chapter 4: Lunch Options

Simple and Quick Salads

21. Quinoa and Kale Salad

Preparation Time: 15 minutes | **Cooking Time:** 15 minutes | **Serving Size:** 2

Ingredients:
- 1 cup quinoa
- 2 cups water
- 2 cups kale, chopped
- 1 avocado, diced
- 1/2 cup cherry tomatoes, halved
- 1/4 cup red onion, finely chopped
- 1/4 cup almonds, sliced
- 2 tablespoons lemon juice
- 2 tablespoons olive oil
- Salt and pepper to taste

Mode of cooking:
- Boiling and assembling

Procedure:
1. Rinse the quinoa under cold water. In a medium saucepan, bring the water to a boil, add the quinoa, reduce the heat, and simmer for 15 minutes until the water is absorbed. Fluff with a fork and let cool.
2. While the quinoa is cooking, prepare the kale by removing the stems and chopping the leaves into bite-sized pieces.
3. In a large bowl, combine the kale with lemon juice and a pinch of salt. Massage the kale for about 2 minutes to soften it.
4. Add the cooled quinoa, diced avocado, cherry tomatoes, red onion, and sliced almonds to the kale.

5. Drizzle with olive oil, and season with salt and pepper to taste. Toss everything together and serve immediately.

Nutrition (Per serving): Calories: 350 | Fat: 18g | Carbs: 40g | Protein: 10g | Sugar: 3g | Sodium: 70mg

22. Chickpea and Spinach Salad

Preparation Time: 10 minutes | **Cooking Time:** 0 minutes | **Serving Size:** 2

Ingredients:
- 1 can chickpeas, drained and rinsed
- 2 cups baby spinach
- 1/2 red bell pepper, chopped
- 1/4 cup red onion, sliced thinly
- 1/4 cup feta cheese, crumbled
- 2 tablespoons olive oil
- 2 tablespoons balsamic vinegar
- Salt and pepper to taste

Mode of cooking:
- Assembling

Procedure:
1. Drain and rinse the chickpeas. In a large salad bowl, combine the chickpeas and baby spinach.
2. Chop the red bell pepper and thinly slice the red onion. Add them to the salad bowl.
3. Crumble the feta cheese over the salad.
4. Drizzle with olive oil and balsamic vinegar. Season with salt and pepper to taste.
5. Toss the salad until all ingredients are well combined. Serve immediately.

Nutrition (Per serving): Calories: 280 | Fat: 14g | Carbs: 30g | Protein: 10g | Sugar: 6g | Sodium: 320mg

23. Avocado and Tomato Salad

Preparation Time: 10 minutes | **Cooking Time:** 0 minutes | **Serving Size:** 2

Ingredients:
- 2 avocados, diced
- 2 large tomatoes, chopped
- 1/4 cup red onion, finely chopped
- 1/4 cup fresh cilantro, chopped
- 2 tablespoons lime juice
- 1 tablespoon olive oil
- Salt and pepper to taste

Mode of cooking:
- Assembling

Procedure:
1. Dice the avocados and chop the tomatoes. Place them in a large salad bowl.
2. Finely chop the red onion and fresh cilantro. Add to the bowl.
3. Drizzle with lime juice and olive oil.
4. Season with salt and pepper to taste.
5. Gently toss the salad to combine all ingredients. Serve immediately.

Nutrition (Per serving): Calories: 300 | Fat: 24g | Carbs: 22g | Protein: 4g | Sugar: 6g | Sodium: 20mg

24. Mediterranean Cucumber Salad

Preparation Time: 10 minutes | **Cooking Time:** 0 minutes | **Serving Size:** 2

Ingredients:
- 2 cucumbers, diced
- 1/2 cup cherry tomatoes, halved
- 1/4 cup red onion, thinly sliced
- 1/4 cup kalamata olives, pitted and sliced
- 1/4 cup feta cheese, crumbled
- 2 tablespoons olive oil
- 2 tablespoons red wine vinegar
- 1 teaspoon dried oregano
- Salt and pepper to taste

Mode of cooking:
- Assembling

Procedure:
1. Dice the cucumbers and halve the cherry tomatoes. Place them in a large salad bowl.
2. Thinly slice the red onion and kalamata olives. Add to the bowl.
3. Crumble the feta cheese over the salad.
4. Drizzle with olive oil and red wine vinegar. Add dried oregano.
5. Season with salt and pepper to taste. Toss gently to combine all ingredients. Serve immediately.

Nutrition (Per serving): Calories: 250 | Fat: 20g | Carbs: 12g | Protein: 6g | Sugar: 5g | Sodium: 340mg

25. Beet and Walnut Salad

Preparation Time: 15 minutes | **Cooking Time:** 0 minutes | **Serving Size:** 2

Ingredients:
- 2 medium beets, cooked and diced
- 2 cups arugula
- 1/4 cup walnuts, chopped
- 1/4 cup goat cheese, crumbled
- 2 tablespoons olive oil
- 2 tablespoons balsamic vinegar
- Salt and pepper to taste

Mode of cooking:
- Assembling

Procedure:
1. Cook the beets until tender, then dice them into bite-sized pieces.
2. In a large bowl, combine the arugula and diced beets.
3. Chop the walnuts and crumble the goat cheese. Add them to the bowl.
4. Drizzle with olive oil and balsamic vinegar.
5. Season with salt and pepper to taste. Toss gently to combine and serve.

Nutrition (Per serving): Calories: 320 | Fat: 22g | Carbs: 22g | Protein: 8g | Sugar: 14g | Sodium: 180mg

26. Apple and Pecan Salad

Preparation Time: 10 minutes | **Cooking Time:** 0 minutes | **Serving Size:** 2

Ingredients:
- 2 cups mixed greens
- 1 apple, thinly sliced
- 1/4 cup pecans, toasted
- 1/4 cup blue cheese, crumbled
- 2 tablespoons olive oil
- 2 tablespoons apple cider vinegar
- 1 teaspoon Dijon mustard

- Salt and pepper to taste

Mode of cooking:
- Assembling

Procedure:
1. Thinly slice the apple and toast the pecans in a dry skillet until fragrant.
2. In a large salad bowl, combine the mixed greens, sliced apple, and toasted pecans.
3. Crumble the blue cheese over the salad.
4. In a small bowl, whisk together the olive oil, apple cider vinegar, Dijon mustard, salt, and pepper.
5. Drizzle the dressing over the salad. Toss gently to combine and serve immediately.

Nutrition (Per serving): Calories: 280 | Fat: 20g | Carbs: 20g | Protein: 6g | Sugar: 12g | Sodium: 200mg

27. Lentil and Arugula Salad

Preparation Time: 10 minutes | **Cooking Time:** 20 minutes | **Serving Size:** 2

Ingredients:
- 1 cup lentils
- 3 cups water
- 2 cups arugula
- 1/2 cup cherry tomatoes, halved
- 1/4 cup red onion, finely chopped
- 2 tablespoons olive oil
- 2 tablespoons lemon juice
- Salt and pepper to taste

Mode of cooking:
- Boiling and assembling

Procedure:
1. Rinse the lentils under cold water. In a medium saucepan, bring the water to a boil, add the lentils, reduce the heat, and simmer for 20 minutes until tender. Drain and let cool.
2. In a large salad bowl, combine the arugula and cooled lentils.
3. Halve the cherry tomatoes and finely chop the red onion. Add them to the bowl.
4. Drizzle with olive oil and lemon juice.

5. Season with salt and pepper to taste. Toss gently to combine and serve.

Nutrition (Per serving): Calories: 320 | Fat: 10g | Carbs: 40g | Protein: 14g | Sugar: 4g | Sodium: 60mg

28.   Strawberry and Spinach Salad

Preparation Time: 10 minutes | **Cooking Time:** 0 minutes | **Serving Size:** 2

Ingredients:
- 2 cups baby spinach
- 1 cup strawberries, sliced
- 1/4 cup red onion, thinly sliced
- 1/4 cup almonds, sliced
- 2 tablespoons balsamic vinegar
- 2 tablespoons olive oil
- 1 teaspoon honey
- Salt and pepper to taste

Mode of cooking:
- Assembling

Procedure:
1. Slice the strawberries and thinly slice the red onion.
2. In a large salad bowl, combine the baby spinach, sliced strawberries, and red onion.
3. Add the sliced almonds to the salad.
4. In a small bowl, whisk together the balsamic vinegar, olive oil, honey, salt, and pepper.
5. Drizzle the dressing over the salad. Toss gently to combine and serve immediately.

Nutrition (Per serving): Calories: 250 | Fat: 16g | Carbs: 24g | Protein: 5g | Sugar: 14g | Sodium: 20mg

29. Mango and Avocado Salad

Preparation Time: 10 minutes | **Cooking Time:** 0 minutes | **Serving Size:** 2

Ingredients:
- 1 mango, diced
- 1 avocado, diced
- 2 cups mixed greens
- 1/4 cup red bell pepper, chopped
- 2 tablespoons lime juice
- 1 tablespoon olive oil
- Salt and pepper to taste

Mode of cooking:
- Assembling

Procedure:
1. Dice the mango and avocado.
2. In a large salad bowl, combine the mixed greens, diced mango, and avocado.
3. Chop the red bell pepper and add to the bowl.
4. Drizzle with lime juice and olive oil.
5. Season with salt and pepper to taste. Toss gently to combine and serve.

Nutrition (Per serving): Calories: 280 | Fat: 20g | Carbs: 28g | Protein: 4g | Sugar: 14g | Sodium: 15mg

30. Broccoli and Quinoa Salad

Preparation Time: 15 minutes | **Cooking Time:** 15 minutes | **Serving Size:** 2

Ingredients:
- 1 cup quinoa
- 2 cups water
- 1 cup broccoli florets, steamed
- 1/2 cup red bell pepper, chopped
- 1/4 cup sunflower seeds
- 2 tablespoons olive oil
- 2 tablespoons apple cider vinegar

- Salt and pepper to taste

Mode of cooking:
- Boiling and assembling

Procedure:
1. Rinse the quinoa under cold water. In a medium saucepan, bring the water to a boil, add the quinoa, reduce the heat, and simmer for 15 minutes until the water is absorbed. Fluff with a fork and let cool.
2. Steam the broccoli florets until tender-crisp.
3. In a large salad bowl, combine the cooled quinoa, steamed broccoli, and chopped red bell pepper.
4. Add the sunflower seeds to the bowl.
5. Drizzle with olive oil and apple cider vinegar. Season with salt and pepper to taste. Toss gently to combine and serve.

Nutrition (Per serving): Calories: 330 | Fat: 16g | Carbs: 38g | Protein: 10g | Sugar: 6g | Sodium: 50mg

Satisfying Soups and Stews

31.   Sweet Potato and Lentil Soup

Preparation Time: 10 minutes | **Cooking Time:** 30 minutes | **Serving Size:** 2

Ingredients:
- 1 large sweet potato, peeled and diced
- 1 cup red lentils, rinsed
- 4 cups vegetable broth
- 1 cup spinach leaves
- 1 teaspoon turmeric powder
- 1 teaspoon ground cumin
- 1 teaspoon ground coriander
- Salt and pepper to taste

Mode of cooking:
- Boiling and simmering

Procedure:
1. In a large pot, add the vegetable broth and bring to a boil.
2. Add the diced sweet potato and rinsed lentils to the pot.
3. Stir in the turmeric, cumin, and coriander. Reduce the heat and let it simmer for 25 minutes.
4. Add the spinach leaves to the pot and cook for an additional 5 minutes until wilted.
5. Season with salt and pepper to taste. Serve hot.

Nutrition (Per serving): Calories: 320 | Fat: 2g | Carbs: 60g | Protein: 14g | Sugar: 10g | Sodium: 700mg

32.   Carrot Ginger Soup

Preparation Time: 10 minutes | **Cooking Time:** 25 minutes | **Serving Size:** 2

Ingredients:
- 4 large carrots, peeled and chopped
- 1 inch fresh ginger, peeled and sliced
- 3 cups vegetable broth
- 1 cup coconut milk
- 1 teaspoon turmeric powder
- Salt and pepper to taste

Mode of cooking:
- Boiling and blending

Procedure:
1. In a large pot, combine the vegetable broth, chopped carrots, and sliced ginger.
2. Bring to a boil, then reduce the heat and let it simmer for 20 minutes until the carrots are tender.
3. Stir in the coconut milk and turmeric powder.
4. Use an immersion blender to puree the soup until smooth.
5. Season with salt and pepper to taste. Serve warm.

Nutrition (Per serving): Calories: 250 | Fat: 10g | Carbs: 35g | Protein: 4g | Sugar: 12g | Sodium: 600mg

33. Chickpea and Spinach Stew

Preparation Time: 10 minutes | **Cooking Time:** 30 minutes | **Serving Size:** 2

Ingredients:
- 1 can chickpeas, drained and rinsed
- 2 cups spinach leaves
- 2 cups vegetable broth
- 1 can diced tomatoes
- 1 teaspoon ground cumin
- 1 teaspoon paprika
- 1 teaspoon garlic powder
- Salt and pepper to taste

Mode of cooking:
- Boiling and simmering

Procedure:
1. In a large pot, combine the vegetable broth and diced tomatoes. Bring to a boil.
2. Add the chickpeas, cumin, paprika, and garlic powder to the pot.
3. Reduce the heat and let it simmer for 25 minutes.
4. Add the spinach leaves and cook for an additional 5 minutes until wilted.
5. Season with salt and pepper to taste. Serve hot.

Nutrition (Per serving): Calories: 280 | Fat: 5g | Carbs: 45g | Protein: 12g | Sugar: 8g | Sodium: 750mg

34. Butternut Squash and Apple Soup

Preparation Time: 10 minutes | **Cooking Time:** 30 minutes | **Serving Size:** 2

Ingredients:
- 1 medium butternut squash, peeled and cubed
- 1 apple, peeled and chopped
- 3 cups vegetable broth
- 1 cup coconut milk
- 1 teaspoon ground cinnamon
- Salt and pepper to taste

Mode of cooking:
- Boiling and blending

Procedure:
1. In a large pot, combine the vegetable broth, butternut squash, and chopped apple.
2. Bring to a boil, then reduce the heat and let it simmer for 25 minutes until the squash is tender.
3. Stir in the coconut milk and ground cinnamon.
4. Use an immersion blender to puree the soup until smooth.
5. Season with salt and pepper to taste. Serve warm.

Nutrition (Per serving): Calories: 300 | Fat: 10g | Carbs: 50g | Protein: 4g | Sugar: 15g | Sodium: 600mg

35. Red Lentil and Tomato Stew

Preparation Time: 10 minutes | **Cooking Time:** 30 minutes | **Serving Size:** 2

Ingredients:
- 1 cup red lentils, rinsed
- 1 can diced tomatoes
- 3 cups vegetable broth
- 1 teaspoon ground cumin
- 1 teaspoon paprika
- 1 teaspoon turmeric powder
- Salt and pepper to taste

Mode of cooking:
- Boiling and simmering

Procedure:
1. In a large pot, combine the vegetable broth and diced tomatoes. Bring to a boil.
2. Add the red lentils, cumin, paprika, and turmeric powder to the pot.
3. Reduce the heat and let it simmer for 30 minutes until the lentils are tender.
4. Stir occasionally to prevent sticking.
5. Season with salt and pepper to taste. Serve hot.

Nutrition (Per serving): Calories: 290 | Fat: 3g | Carbs: 45g | Protein: 16g | Sugar: 8g | Sodium: 700mg

36.   Green Pea and Mint Soup

Preparation Time: 10 minutes | **Cooking Time:** 20 minutes | **Serving Size:** 2

Ingredients:
- 2 cups frozen green peas
- 1 cup fresh mint leaves
- 3 cups vegetable broth
- 1/2 cup coconut milk
- 1 teaspoon garlic powder
- Salt and pepper to taste

Mode of cooking:
- Boiling and blending

Procedure:
1. In a large pot, combine the vegetable broth and green peas. Bring to a boil.
2. Reduce the heat and let it simmer for 15 minutes until the peas are tender.
3. Add the fresh mint leaves and coconut milk to the pot.
4. Use an immersion blender to puree the soup until smooth.
5. Season with garlic powder, salt, and pepper to taste. Serve warm.

Nutrition (Per serving): Calories: 240 | Fat: 8g | Carbs: 35g | Protein: 6g | Sugar: 6g | Sodium: 500mg

37.   Turmeric Cauliflower Soup

Preparation Time: 10 minutes | **Cooking Time:** 25 minutes | **Serving Size:** 2

Ingredients:
- 1 head of cauliflower, chopped
- 3 cups vegetable broth
- 1 cup coconut milk
- 1 teaspoon turmeric powder
- 1 teaspoon ground ginger
- Salt and pepper to taste

Mode of cooking:
- Boiling and blending

Procedure:
1. In a large pot, combine the vegetable broth and chopped cauliflower. Bring to a boil.
2. Reduce the heat and let it simmer for 20 minutes until the cauliflower is tender.
3. Stir in the coconut milk, turmeric powder, and ground ginger.
4. Use an immersion blender to puree the soup until smooth.
5. Season with salt and pepper to taste. Serve warm.

Nutrition (Per serving): Calories: 230 | Fat: 10g | Carbs: 28g | Protein: 5g | Sugar: 6g | Sodium: 600mg

38. Sweet Potato and Black Bean Stew

Preparation Time: 10 minutes | **Cooking Time:** 30 minutes | **Serving Size:** 2

Ingredients:
- 1 large sweet potato, peeled and diced
- 1 can black beans, drained and rinsed
- 3 cups vegetable broth
- 1 can diced tomatoes
- 1 teaspoon ground cumin
- 1 teaspoon paprika
- Salt and pepper to taste

Mode of cooking:
- Boiling and simmering

Procedure:
1. In a large pot, combine the vegetable broth, diced sweet potato, and diced tomatoes. Bring to a boil.
2. Add the black beans, ground cumin, and paprika to the pot.
3. Reduce the heat and let it simmer for 30 minutes until the sweet potato is tender.
4. Stir occasionally to prevent sticking.
5. Season with salt and pepper to taste. Serve hot.

Nutrition (Per serving): Calories: 320 | Fat: 3g | Carbs: 60g | Protein: 12g | Sugar: 8g | Sodium: 700mg

39. Broccoli and White Bean Soup

Preparation Time: 10 minutes | **Cooking Time:** 20 minutes | **Serving Size:** 2

Ingredients:
- 2 cups broccoli florets
- 1 can white beans, drained and rinsed
- 3 cups vegetable broth
- 1 cup coconut milk
- 1 teaspoon garlic powder
- Salt and pepper to taste

Mode of cooking:
- Boiling and blending

Procedure:
1. In a large pot, combine the vegetable broth and broccoli florets. Bring to a boil.
2. Reduce the heat and let it simmer for 15 minutes until the broccoli is tender.
3. Add the white beans and coconut milk to the pot.
4. Use an immersion blender to puree the soup until smooth.
5. Season with garlic powder, salt, and pepper to taste. Serve warm.

Nutrition (Per serving): Calories: 270 | Fat: 8g | Carbs: 35g | Protein: 10g | Sugar: 4g | Sodium: 600mg

40. Zucchini and Basil Soup

Preparation Time: 10 minutes | **Cooking Time:** 25 minutes | **Serving Size:** 2

Ingredients:
- 2 large zucchinis, chopped
- 3 cups vegetable broth
- 1 cup fresh basil leaves
- 1/2 cup coconut milk
- 1 teaspoon garlic powder
- Salt and pepper to taste

Mode of cooking:

- Boiling and blending

Procedure:
1. In a large pot, combine the vegetable broth and chopped zucchinis. Bring to a boil.
2. Reduce the heat and let it simmer for 20 minutes until the zucchinis are tender.
3. Add the fresh basil leaves and coconut milk to the pot.
4. Use an immersion blender to puree the soup until smooth.
5. Season with garlic powder, salt, and pepper to taste. Serve warm.

Nutrition (Per serving): Calories: 230 | Fat: 8g | Carbs: 28g | Protein: 4g | Sugar: 6g | Sodium: 600mg

Chapter 5: Dinner Recipes

Light and Delicious Dinner Dishes

41.   Baked Lemon Herb Salmon

Preparation Time: 10 minutes | **Cooking Time:** 20 minutes | **Serving Size:** 2

Ingredients:
- 2 salmon fillets
- 1 lemon, sliced
- 2 tablespoons fresh dill, chopped
- 1 tablespoon olive oil
- Salt and pepper to taste

Mode of cooking:
- Baking

Procedure:
1. Preheat the oven to 375°F (190°C).
2. Place the salmon fillets on a baking sheet lined with parchment paper.
3. Drizzle olive oil over the salmon and season with salt and pepper.
4. Top each fillet with lemon slices and sprinkle with fresh dill.
5. Bake for 20 minutes or until the salmon is cooked through and flakes easily with a fork. Serve warm.

Nutrition (Per serving): Calories: 350 | Fat: 20g | Carbs: 2g | Protein: 35g | Sugar: 0g | Sodium: 60mg

42. Quinoa Stuffed Bell Peppers

Preparation Time: 15 minutes | **Cooking Time:** 30 minutes | **Serving Size:** 2

Ingredients:
- 2 bell peppers, halved and seeded
- 1 cup cooked quinoa
- 1/2 cup black beans, drained and rinsed
- 1/2 cup corn kernels
- 1/2 cup cherry tomatoes, halved
- 1/4 cup cilantro, chopped
- 1 tablespoon lime juice
- Salt and pepper to taste

Mode of cooking:
- Baking

Procedure:
1. Preheat the oven to 375°F (190°C).
2. In a mixing bowl, combine cooked quinoa, black beans, corn, cherry tomatoes, cilantro, lime juice, salt, and pepper.
3. Stuff the bell pepper halves with the quinoa mixture.
4. Place the stuffed peppers in a baking dish and cover with aluminum foil.
5. Bake for 30 minutes or until the peppers are tender. Serve warm.

Nutrition (Per serving): Calories: 280 | Fat: 6g | Carbs: 45g | Protein: 10g | Sugar: 8g | Sodium: 300mg

43. Zucchini Noodles with Pesto

Preparation Time: 10 minutes | **Cooking Time:** 5 minutes | **Serving Size:** 2

Ingredients:
- 2 large zucchinis, spiralized
- 1/4 cup basil pesto
- 1/4 cup cherry tomatoes, halved
- 2 tablespoons pine nuts
- Salt and pepper to taste

Mode of cooking:
- Sautéing (without oil)

Procedure:
1. Spiralize the zucchinis into noodles using a spiralizer.
2. In a large non-stick skillet, add the zucchini noodles and cook over medium heat for 3-4 minutes until just tender.
3. Remove the skillet from heat and stir in the basil pesto.
4. Add the cherry tomatoes and pine nuts to the skillet.
5. Season with salt and pepper to taste. Serve immediately.

Nutrition (Per serving): Calories: 200 | Fat: 14g | Carbs: 16g | Protein: 4g | Sugar: 6g | Sodium: 150mg

44. Baked Cod with Asparagus

Preparation Time: 10 minutes | **Cooking Time:** 20 minutes | **Serving Size:** 2

Ingredients:
- 2 cod fillets
- 1 bunch asparagus, trimmed
- 2 tablespoons olive oil
- 1 lemon, sliced
- 1 tablespoon fresh parsley, chopped
- Salt and pepper to taste

Mode of cooking:

- Baking

Procedure:
1. Preheat the oven to 375°F (190°C).
2. Place the cod fillets and asparagus on a baking sheet lined with parchment paper.
3. Drizzle with olive oil and season with salt and pepper.
4. Top the cod with lemon slices and sprinkle with fresh parsley.
5. Bake for 20 minutes or until the cod is cooked through and the asparagus is tender. Serve warm.

Nutrition (Per serving): Calories: 300 | Fat: 14g | Carbs: 10g | Protein: 34g | Sugar: 3g | Sodium: 120mg

45. Chickpea and Spinach Curry

Preparation Time: 10 minutes | **Cooking Time:** 20 minutes | **Serving Size:** 2

Ingredients:
- 1 can chickpeas, drained and rinsed
- 2 cups spinach leaves
- 1 cup coconut milk
- 1/2 cup diced tomatoes
- 1 tablespoon curry powder
- 1 teaspoon ground cumin
- Salt and pepper to taste

Mode of cooking:
- Simmering

Procedure:
1. In a large pot, combine chickpeas, spinach, coconut milk, and diced tomatoes.
2. Stir in curry powder and ground cumin.
3. Bring to a simmer over medium heat and cook for 15-20 minutes until the spinach is wilted and the flavors are combined.
4. Season with salt and pepper to taste.
5. Serve hot with a side of quinoa or brown rice.

Nutrition (Per serving): Calories: 320 | Fat: 14g | Carbs: 38g | Protein: 12g | Sugar: 8g | Sodium: 400mg

46. Lemon Herb Chicken and Vegetables

Preparation Time: 15 minutes | **Cooking Time:** 30 minutes | **Serving Size:** 2

Ingredients:
- 2 chicken breasts
- 1 cup baby carrots
- 1 cup broccoli florets
- 1 lemon, juiced
- 2 tablespoons olive oil
- 1 tablespoon fresh rosemary, chopped
- Salt and pepper to taste

Mode of cooking:
- Baking

Procedure:
1. Preheat the oven to 375°F (190°C).
2. Place the chicken breasts, baby carrots, and broccoli florets in a baking dish.
3. Drizzle with olive oil and lemon juice, and sprinkle with fresh rosemary, salt, and pepper.
4. Cover the dish with aluminum foil and bake for 30 minutes or until the chicken is cooked through and the vegetables are tender.
5. Serve warm, ensuring each plate has a portion of chicken and vegetables.

Nutrition (Per serving): Calories: 340 | Fat: 15g | Carbs: 12g | Protein: 40g | Sugar: 6g | Sodium: 150mg

47. Spaghetti Squash with Tomato Basil Sauce

Preparation Time: 15 minutes | **Cooking Time:** 40 minutes | **Serving Size:** 2

Ingredients:
- 1 medium spaghetti squash
- 1 cup cherry tomatoes, halved
- 1/4 cup fresh basil, chopped
- 2 cloves garlic, minced
- 1 tablespoon olive oil
- Salt and pepper to taste

Mode of cooking:
- Baking and simmering

Procedure:
1. Preheat the oven to 375°F (190°C).
2. Cut the spaghetti squash in half lengthwise and remove the seeds. Place cut-side down on a baking sheet lined with parchment paper.
3. Bake for 35-40 minutes until the squash is tender. Use a fork to scrape the flesh into spaghetti-like strands.
4. In a large pot, heat the olive oil over medium heat. Add the minced garlic and cook for 1 minute until fragrant.
5. Add the cherry tomatoes and cook for 5-7 minutes until they begin to break down. Stir in the fresh basil, salt, and pepper.
6. Combine the spaghetti squash strands with the tomato basil sauce. Serve warm.

Nutrition (Per serving): Calories: 240 | Fat: 9g | Carbs: 36g | Protein: 4g | Sugar: 12g | Sodium: 120mg

48. Mediterranean Chickpea Salad

Preparation Time: 15 minutes | **Cooking Time:** 0 minutes | **Serving Size:** 2

Ingredients:
- 1 can chickpeas, drained and rinsed
- 1/2 cup cherry tomatoes, halved
- 1/4 cup cucumber, diced
- 1/4 cup red onion, finely chopped
- 1/4 cup kalamata olives, sliced
- 2 tablespoons olive oil
- 1 tablespoon red wine vinegar
- 1 tablespoon fresh parsley, chopped
- Salt and pepper to taste

Mode of cooking:
- Assembling

Procedure:
1. In a large bowl, combine chickpeas, cherry tomatoes, cucumber, red onion, and kalamata olives.
2. Drizzle with olive oil and red wine vinegar.
3. Sprinkle with fresh parsley, salt, and pepper.
4. Toss gently to combine all ingredients.
5. Serve immediately or refrigerate for 30 minutes to let the flavors meld.

Nutrition (Per serving): Calories: 280 | Fat: 14g | Carbs: 32g | Protein: 8g | Sugar: 6g | Sodium: 250mg

49.   Baked Eggplant Parmesan

Preparation Time: 20 minutes | **Cooking Time:** 40 minutes | **Serving Size:** 2

Ingredients:
- 1 large eggplant, sliced
- 1 cup marinara sauce
- 1/2 cup mozzarella cheese, shredded
- 1/4 cup Parmesan cheese, grated
- 1 tablespoon olive oil
- 1 teaspoon dried oregano
- Salt and pepper to taste

Mode of cooking:
- Baking

Procedure:
1. Preheat the oven to 375°F (190°C).
2. Place the eggplant slices on a baking sheet lined with parchment paper. Drizzle with olive oil and season with salt and pepper.
3. Bake for 20 minutes, turning once halfway through, until tender.
4. In a baking dish, spread a layer of marinara sauce, then a layer of eggplant slices. Repeat layers, ending with marinara sauce on top.
5. Sprinkle with mozzarella cheese, Parmesan cheese, and dried oregano.
6. Bake for an additional 20 minutes until the cheese is melted and bubbly. Serve warm.

Nutrition (Per serving): Calories: 320 | Fat: 18g | Carbs: 28g | Protein: 12g | Sugar: 10g | Sodium: 450mg

50. Lemon Garlic Shrimp and Zoodles

Preparation Time: 15 minutes | **Cooking Time:** 10 minutes | **Serving Size:** 2

Ingredients:
- 1 lb large shrimp, peeled and deveined
- 2 large zucchinis, spiralized
- 2 cloves garlic, minced
- 1 lemon, juiced
- 2 tablespoons olive oil
- Salt and pepper to taste
- 1 tablespoon fresh parsley, chopped

Mode of cooking:
- Sautéing (without oil)

Procedure:
1. Spiralize the zucchinis into noodles using a spiralizer.
2. In a large non-stick skillet, add the zucchini noodles and cook over medium heat for 3-4 minutes until just tender. Remove and set aside.
3. In the same skillet, add the minced garlic and cook for 1 minute until fragrant.
4. Add the shrimp, lemon juice, olive oil, salt, and pepper. Cook for 3-4 minutes until the shrimp are pink and opaque.
5. Return the zucchini noodles to the skillet and toss to combine with the shrimp and garlic. Sprinkle with fresh parsley and serve warm.

Nutrition (Per serving): Calories: 270 | Fat: 14g | Carbs: 8g | Protein: 28g | Sugar: 4g | Sodium: 400mg

51. Grilled Chicken with Mango Salsa

Preparation Time: 15 minutes | **Cooking Time:** 20 minutes | **Serving Size:** 2

Ingredients:
- 2 chicken breasts
- 1 mango, diced
- 1/2 red bell pepper, diced
- 1/4 cup red onion, finely chopped
- 1/4 cup fresh cilantro, chopped
- 1 lime, juiced
- 2 tablespoons olive oil
- Salt and pepper to taste

Mode of cooking:
- Grilling

Procedure:
1. Preheat the grill to medium-high heat.
2. Season the chicken breasts with salt, pepper, and 1 tablespoon of olive oil.
3. Grill the chicken for 6-7 minutes on each side until fully cooked.
4. While the chicken is grilling, prepare the mango salsa by combining diced mango, red bell pepper, red onion, fresh cilantro, lime juice, and the remaining olive oil in a bowl. Mix well.
5. Serve the grilled chicken topped with mango salsa.

Nutrition (Per serving): Calories: 350 | Fat: 14g | Carbs: 18g | Protein: 38g | Sugar: 14g | Sodium: 200mg

52. Stuffed Portobello Mushrooms

Preparation Time: 15 minutes | **Cooking Time:** 25 minutes | **Serving Size:** 2

Ingredients:
- 4 large Portobello mushrooms
- 1 cup quinoa, cooked
- 1/2 cup spinach, chopped
- 1/4 cup sun-dried tomatoes, chopped
- 1/4 cup feta cheese, crumbled
- 1 tablespoon olive oil
- Salt and pepper to taste

Mode of cooking:
- Baking

Procedure:
1. Preheat the oven to 375°F (190°C).
2. Clean the Portobello mushrooms and remove the stems.
3. In a mixing bowl, combine cooked quinoa, chopped spinach, sun-dried tomatoes, feta cheese, olive oil, salt, and pepper.
4. Stuff each mushroom cap with the quinoa mixture.
5. Place the stuffed mushrooms on a baking sheet and bake for 25 minutes until the mushrooms are tender and the stuffing is heated through. Serve warm.

Nutrition (Per serving): Calories: 280 | Fat: 10g | Carbs: 34g | Protein: 12g | Sugar: 6g | Sodium: 300mg

53. Baked Tilapia with Lemon and Dill

Preparation Time: 10 minutes | **Cooking Time:** 20 minutes | **Serving Size:** 2

Ingredients:
- 2 tilapia fillets
- 1 lemon, sliced
- 2 tablespoons fresh dill, chopped
- 1 tablespoon olive oil
- Salt and pepper to taste

Mode of cooking:
- Baking

Procedure:
1. Preheat the oven to 375°F (190°C).
2. Place the tilapia fillets on a baking sheet lined with parchment paper.
3. Drizzle with olive oil and season with salt and pepper.
4. Top each fillet with lemon slices and sprinkle with fresh dill.
5. Bake for 20 minutes or until the tilapia is cooked through and flakes easily with a fork. Serve warm.

Nutrition (Per serving): Calories: 280 | Fat: 12g | Carbs: 2g | Protein: 38g | Sugar: 0g | Sodium: 120mg

54. Vegan Lentil Shepherd's Pie

Preparation Time: 20 minutes | **Cooking Time:** 40 minutes | **Serving Size:** 2

Ingredients:
- 1 cup lentils, cooked
- 2 cups mashed potatoes
- 1/2 cup carrots, diced
- 1/2 cup peas
- 1/2 cup corn kernels
- 1 cup vegetable broth
- 1 tablespoon olive oil
- 1 teaspoon garlic powder
- Salt and pepper to taste

Mode of cooking:
- Baking

Procedure:
1. Preheat the oven to 375°F (190°C).
2. In a mixing bowl, combine cooked lentils, diced carrots, peas, corn, vegetable broth, olive oil, garlic powder, salt, and pepper.
3. Spread the lentil mixture in a baking dish.

4. Top with mashed potatoes, spreading them evenly over the lentil mixture.
5. Bake for 40 minutes until the top is golden and the filling is bubbly. Serve warm.

Nutrition (Per serving): Calories: 350 | Fat: 10g | Carbs: 55g | Protein: 12g | Sugar: 6g | Sodium: 350mg

55. Roasted Vegetable and Chickpea Bowl

Preparation Time: 15 minutes | **Cooking Time:** 25 minutes | **Serving Size:** 2

Ingredients:
- 1 cup chickpeas, drained and rinsed
- 1 cup cherry tomatoes, halved
- 1 zucchini, sliced
- 1 bell pepper, diced
- 1 tablespoon olive oil
- 1 teaspoon paprika
- 1 teaspoon garlic powder
- Salt and pepper to taste

Mode of cooking:
- Roasting

Procedure:
1. Preheat the oven to 400°F (200°C).
2. In a large mixing bowl, combine chickpeas, cherry tomatoes, zucchini, bell pepper, olive oil, paprika, garlic powder, salt, and pepper.
3. Spread the mixture on a baking sheet lined with parchment paper.
4. Roast for 25 minutes until the vegetables are tender and slightly caramelized.
5. Serve warm in bowls, optionally over a bed of greens or quinoa.

Nutrition (Per serving): Calories: 300 | Fat: 12g | Carbs: 38g | Protein: 10g | Sugar: 8g | Sodium: 300mg

Fish and Seafood for Beginners

56.   Baked Garlic Butter Shrimp

Preparation Time: 10 minutes | **Cooking Time:** 15 minutes | **Serving Size:** 2

Ingredients:
- 1 lb shrimp, peeled and deveined
- 2 tablespoons unsalted butter, melted
- 2 cloves garlic, minced
- 1 lemon, sliced
- 1 tablespoon fresh parsley, chopped
- Salt and pepper to taste

Mode of cooking:
- Baking

Procedure:
1. Preheat the oven to 375°F (190°C).
2. Arrange the shrimp in a single layer on a baking sheet.
3. In a small bowl, mix melted butter, minced garlic, salt, and pepper.
4. Drizzle the garlic butter over the shrimp, then top with lemon slices.
5. Bake for 15 minutes until the shrimp are pink and opaque. Garnish with fresh parsley before serving.

Nutrition (Per serving): Calories: 280 | Fat: 14g | Carbs: 2g | Protein: 35g | Sugar: 0g | Sodium: 600mg

57. Herb-Crusted Salmon

Preparation Time: 10 minutes | **Cooking Time:** 20 minutes | **Serving Size:** 2

Ingredients:
- 2 salmon fillets
- 1 tablespoon Dijon mustard
- 2 tablespoons breadcrumbs
- 2 tablespoons fresh dill, chopped
- 1 tablespoon olive oil
- Salt and pepper to taste

Mode of cooking:
- Baking

Procedure:
1. Preheat the oven to 375°F (190°C).
2. Place the salmon fillets on a baking sheet lined with parchment paper.
3. Spread Dijon mustard evenly over the top of each fillet.
4. In a small bowl, mix breadcrumbs, fresh dill, olive oil, salt, and pepper.
5. Press the breadcrumb mixture onto the mustard-coated salmon. Bake for 20 minutes until the salmon is cooked through and the topping is golden brown.

Nutrition (Per serving): Calories: 360 | Fat: 20g | Carbs: 8g | Protein: 34g | Sugar: 0g | Sodium: 280mg

58. Lemon Herb Tilapia

Preparation Time: 10 minutes | **Cooking Time:** 15 minutes | **Serving Size:** 2

Ingredients:
- 2 tilapia fillets
- 1 lemon, juiced
- 1 tablespoon olive oil
- 1 teaspoon dried thyme
- 1 teaspoon dried basil
- Salt and pepper to taste

Mode of cooking:
- Baking

Procedure:
1. Preheat the oven to 375°F (190°C).
2. Place the tilapia fillets on a baking sheet lined with parchment paper.
3. Drizzle with olive oil and lemon juice, and season with thyme, basil, salt, and pepper.
4. Bake for 15 minutes until the tilapia is cooked through and flakes easily with a fork. Serve warm.

Nutrition (Per serving): Calories: 240 | Fat: 10g | Carbs: 2g | Protein: 36g | Sugar: 0g | Sodium: 100mg

59. Baked Cod with Tomato Basil Sauce

Preparation Time: 15 minutes | **Cooking Time:** 25 minutes | **Serving Size:** 2

Ingredients:
- 2 cod fillets
- 1 cup cherry tomatoes, halved
- 2 cloves garlic, minced
- 1/4 cup fresh basil, chopped
- 1 tablespoon olive oil
- Salt and pepper to taste

Mode of cooking:
- Baking

Procedure:
1. Preheat the oven to 375°F (190°C).
2. In a small bowl, mix cherry tomatoes, garlic, basil, olive oil, salt, and pepper.
3. Place the cod fillets in a baking dish and top with the tomato basil mixture.
4. Cover the dish with aluminum foil and bake for 25 minutes until the cod is cooked through.
5. Serve warm, garnished with additional fresh basil if desired.

Nutrition (Per serving): Calories: 280 | Fat: 12g | Carbs: 6g | Protein: 36g | Sugar: 3g | Sodium: 200mg

60.   Garlic Lemon Shrimp Skewers

Preparation Time: 15 minutes | **Cooking Time:** 10 minutes | **Serving Size:** 2

Ingredients:
- 1 lb large shrimp, peeled and deveined
- 2 tablespoons olive oil
- 2 cloves garlic, minced
- 1 lemon, juiced
- 1 tablespoon fresh parsley, chopped
- Salt and pepper to taste

Mode of cooking:
- Grilling

Procedure:
1. Preheat the grill to medium-high heat.
2. In a bowl, mix olive oil, minced garlic, lemon juice, salt, and pepper.
3. Thread the shrimp onto skewers and brush with the garlic lemon mixture.
4. Grill for 2-3 minutes on each side until the shrimp are pink and cooked through.
5. Garnish with fresh parsley and serve immediately.

Nutrition (Per serving): Calories: 280 | Fat: 12g | Carbs: 3g | Protein: 36g | Sugar: 0g | Sodium: 600mg

61. Baked Scallops with Lemon Butter

Preparation Time: 10 minutes | **Cooking Time:** 15 minutes | **Serving Size:** 2

Ingredients:
- 1 lb scallops
- 2 tablespoons unsalted butter, melted
- 1 lemon, juiced
- 1 tablespoon fresh parsley, chopped
- Salt and pepper to taste

Mode of cooking:
- Baking

Procedure:
1. Preheat the oven to 375°F (190°C).
2. Arrange the scallops in a single layer in a baking dish.
3. In a small bowl, mix melted butter, lemon juice, salt, and pepper.
4. Pour the lemon butter over the scallops and bake for 15 minutes until the scallops are opaque.
5. Garnish with fresh parsley and serve warm.

Nutrition (Per serving): Calories: 300 | Fat: 14g | Carbs: 3g | Protein: 36g | Sugar: 0g | Sodium: 600mg

62. Baked Halibut with Pesto

Preparation Time: 10 minutes | **Cooking Time:** 20 minutes | **Serving Size:** 2

Ingredients:
- 2 halibut fillets
- 1/4 cup basil pesto
- 1 lemon, sliced
- 1 tablespoon olive oil
- Salt and pepper to taste

Mode of cooking:
- Baking

Procedure:
1. Preheat the oven to 375°F (190°C).
2. Place the halibut fillets on a baking sheet lined with parchment paper.
3. Spread basil pesto evenly over the top of each fillet.
4. Drizzle with olive oil, top with lemon slices, and season with salt and pepper.
5. Bake for 20 minutes until the halibut is cooked through and flakes easily with a fork.

Nutrition (Per serving): Calories: 350 | Fat: 20g | Carbs: 4g | Protein: 36g | Sugar: 0g | Sodium: 280mg

63. Citrus Herb Grilled Salmon

Preparation Time: 15 minutes | **Cooking Time:** 10 minutes | **Serving Size:** 2

Ingredients:
- 2 salmon fillets
- 1 orange, juiced and zested
- 1 lemon, juiced and zested
- 1 tablespoon olive oil
- 1 teaspoon dried thyme
- Salt and pepper to taste

Mode of cooking:
- Grilling

Procedure:
1. Preheat the grill to medium-high heat.
2. In a bowl, mix orange juice, lemon juice, olive oil, thyme, salt, and pepper.
3. Brush the salmon fillets with the citrus herb mixture.
4. Grill the salmon for 4-5 minutes on each side until cooked through.
5. Garnish with orange and lemon zest before serving.

Nutrition (Per serving): Calories: 330 | Fat: 20g | Carbs: 4g | Protein: 34g | Sugar: 2g | Sodium: 180mg

64. Baked Trout with Dill

Preparation Time: 10 minutes | **Cooking Time:** 25 minutes | **Serving Size:** 2

Ingredients:
- 2 trout fillets
- 1 lemon, sliced
- 2 tablespoons fresh dill, chopped
- 1 tablespoon olive oil
- Salt and pepper to taste

Mode of cooking:
- Baking

Procedure:
1. Preheat the oven to 375°F (190°C).
2. Place the trout fillets on a baking sheet lined with parchment paper.
3. Drizzle with olive oil, season with salt and pepper, and sprinkle with fresh dill.
4. Top each fillet with lemon slices.
5. Bake for 25 minutes until the trout is cooked through and flakes easily with a fork. Serve warm.

Nutrition (Per serving): Calories: 320 | Fat: 18g | Carbs: 3g | Protein: 36g | Sugar: 0g | Sodium: 120mg

65. Lemon Herb Baked Haddock

Preparation Time: 10 minutes | **Cooking Time:** 20 minutes | **Serving Size:** 2

Ingredients:
- 2 haddock fillets
- 1 lemon, juiced
- 1 tablespoon olive oil
- 1 teaspoon dried basil
- 1 teaspoon dried thyme
- Salt and pepper to taste

Mode of cooking:
- Baking

Procedure:
1. Preheat the oven to 375°F (190°C).
2. Place the haddock fillets on a baking sheet lined with parchment paper.
3. Drizzle with olive oil and lemon juice, and season with basil, thyme, salt, and pepper.
4. Bake for 20 minutes until the haddock is cooked through and flakes easily with a fork. Serve warm.

Nutrition (Per serving): Calories: 250 | Fat: 10g | Carbs: 2g | Protein: 36g | Sugar: 0g | Sodium: 120mg

66.   Garlic Butter Baked Lobster Tail

Preparation Time: 10 minutes | **Cooking Time:** 15 minutes | **Serving Size:** 2

Ingredients:
- 2 lobster tails
- 2 tablespoons unsalted butter, melted
- 2 cloves garlic, minced
- 1 lemon, juiced
- 1 tablespoon fresh parsley, chopped
- Salt and pepper to taste

Mode of cooking:
- Baking

Procedure:
1. Preheat the oven to 375°F (190°C).
2. Using kitchen shears, cut the top shell of the lobster tails lengthwise and pull the meat out slightly to rest on top.
3. In a small bowl, mix melted butter, minced garlic, lemon juice, salt, and pepper.
4. Brush the garlic butter over the lobster meat.
5. Bake for 15 minutes until the lobster meat is opaque. Garnish with fresh parsley and serve warm.

Nutrition (Per serving): Calories: 280 | Fat: 14g | Carbs: 2g | Protein: 36g | Sugar: 0g | Sodium: 600mg

67. Baked Swordfish with Capers and Olives

Preparation Time: 15 minutes | **Cooking Time:** 25 minutes | **Serving Size:** 2

Ingredients:
- 2 swordfish steaks
- 1/4 cup capers, drained
- 1/4 cup green olives, sliced
- 1 lemon, juiced
- 1 tablespoon olive oil
- 1 teaspoon dried oregano
- Salt and pepper to taste

Mode of cooking:
- Baking

Procedure:
1. Preheat the oven to 375°F (190°C).
2. Place the swordfish steaks in a baking dish.
3. In a small bowl, mix capers, olives, lemon juice, olive oil, oregano, salt, and pepper.
4. Pour the mixture over the swordfish steaks.
5. Bake for 25 minutes until the swordfish is cooked through and flakes easily with a fork. Serve warm.

Nutrition (Per serving): Calories: 360 | Fat: 20g | Carbs: 4g | Protein: 38g | Sugar: 0g | Sodium: 600mg

68. Honey Lime Baked Mahi Mahi

Preparation Time: 10 minutes | **Cooking Time:** 20 minutes | **Serving Size:** 2

Ingredients:
- 2 mahi mahi fillets
- 1 lime, juiced
- 1 tablespoon honey
- 1 tablespoon olive oil
- 1 teaspoon garlic powder
- Salt and pepper to taste

Mode of cooking:
- Baking

Procedure:
1. Preheat the oven to 375°F (190°C).
2. Place the mahi mahi fillets on a baking sheet lined with parchment paper.
3. In a small bowl, mix lime juice, honey, olive oil, garlic powder, salt, and pepper.
4. Brush the honey lime mixture over the fillets.
5. Bake for 20 minutes until the mahi mahi is cooked through and flakes easily with a fork. Serve warm.

Nutrition (Per serving): Calories: 320 | Fat: 12g | Carbs: 8g | Protein: 38g | Sugar: 6g | Sodium: 120mg

69. Sesame Crusted Tuna Steaks

Preparation Time: 15 minutes | **Cooking Time:** 10 minutes | **Serving Size:** 2

Ingredients:
- 2 tuna steaks
- 1/4 cup sesame seeds
- 1 tablespoon olive oil
- 1 tablespoon soy sauce
- 1 tablespoon rice vinegar
- 1 teaspoon fresh ginger, grated
- Salt and pepper to taste

Mode of cooking:
- Grilling

Procedure:
1. Preheat the grill to medium-high heat.
2. In a small bowl, mix soy sauce, rice vinegar, fresh ginger, salt, and pepper.
3. Brush the tuna steaks with the mixture and then coat them with sesame seeds.
4. Grill the tuna steaks for 2-3 minutes on each side until seared on the outside but still pink in the center.
5. Serve warm with a drizzle of any remaining soy sauce mixture.

Nutrition (Per serving): Calories: 340 | Fat: 18g | Carbs: 4g | Protein: 36g | Sugar: 0g | Sodium: 400mg

70. Baked Lemon Garlic Sole

Preparation Time: 10 minutes | **Cooking Time:** 20 minutes | **Serving Size:** 2

Ingredients:
- 2 sole fillets
- 1 lemon, juiced
- 2 cloves garlic, minced
- 1 tablespoon olive oil
- 1 tablespoon fresh parsley, chopped
- Salt and pepper to taste

Mode of cooking:
- Baking

Procedure:
1. Preheat the oven to 375°F (190°C).
2. Place the sole fillets on a baking sheet lined with parchment paper.
3. In a small bowl, mix lemon juice, minced garlic, olive oil, salt, and pepper.
4. Pour the lemon garlic mixture over the sole fillets.
5. Bake for 20 minutes until the sole is cooked through and flakes easily with a fork. Garnish with fresh parsley before serving.

Nutrition (Per serving): Calories: 280 | Fat: 12g | Carbs: 2g | Protein: 38g | Sugar: 0g | Sodium: 200mg

Chapter 6: Snacks and Small Meals

Healthy Snacks for In-Between

71. Apple and Almond Butter Bites

Preparation Time: 10 minutes | **Cooking Time:** 0 minutes | **Serving Size:** 2

Ingredients:
- 1 large apple, sliced
- 4 tablespoons almond butter
- 1 tablespoon chia seeds
- 1 tablespoon honey (optional)
- 1 teaspoon cinnamon

Mode of cooking:
- Assembling

Procedure:
1. Wash and slice the apple into thin rounds.
2. Spread almond butter evenly on each apple slice.
3. Sprinkle chia seeds and cinnamon over the almond butter.
4. Drizzle honey on top if desired.
5. Serve immediately for a quick, nutritious snack.

Nutrition (Per serving): Calories: 210 | Fat: 14g | Carbs: 22g | Protein: 4g | Sugar: 12g | Sodium: 5mg

72. Greek Yogurt Parfait

Preparation Time: 10 minutes | **Cooking Time:** 0 minutes | **Serving Size:** 2

Ingredients:
- 1 cup Greek yogurt
- 1/2 cup mixed berries (blueberries, raspberries, strawberries)
- 1/4 cup granola
- 1 tablespoon honey

- 1 tablespoon flax seeds

Mode of cooking:
- Assembling

Procedure:
1. Divide the Greek yogurt evenly between two bowls.
2. Layer mixed berries on top of the yogurt.
3. Sprinkle granola and flax seeds over the berries.
4. Drizzle honey on top.
5. Serve immediately for a refreshing snack.

Nutrition (Per serving): Calories: 220 | Fat: 8g | Carbs: 30g | Protein: 10g | Sugar: 18g | Sodium: 55mg

73. Avocado Toast

Preparation Time: 5 minutes | **Cooking Time:** 5 minutes | **Serving Size:** 2

Ingredients:
- 2 slices whole grain bread
- 1 ripe avocado
- 1 tablespoon lemon juice
- 1/4 teaspoon red pepper flakes
- Salt and pepper to taste

Mode of cooking:
- Toasting

Procedure:
1. Toast the whole grain bread slices until golden brown.
2. Mash the avocado in a bowl with lemon juice, salt, and pepper.
3. Spread the mashed avocado evenly on each slice of toast.
4. Sprinkle red pepper flakes on top.
5. Serve immediately for a quick and healthy snack.

Nutrition (Per serving): Calories: 240 | Fat: 14g | Carbs: 24g | Protein: 4g | Sugar: 2g | Sodium: 180mg

74. Veggie Sticks with Hummus

Preparation Time: 10 minutes | **Cooking Time:** 0 minutes | **Serving Size:** 2

Ingredients:
- 1 cucumber, sliced into sticks
- 2 carrots, sliced into sticks
- 1 bell pepper, sliced into sticks
- 1 cup hummus

Mode of cooking:
- Assembling

Procedure:
1. Wash and slice the cucumber, carrots, and bell pepper into sticks.
2. Arrange the veggie sticks on a platter.
3. Serve with a cup of hummus for dipping.
4. Enjoy immediately as a healthy snack.

Nutrition (Per serving): Calories: 150 | Fat: 6g | Carbs: 18g | Protein: 4g | Sugar: 6g | Sodium: 300mg

75. Chia Pudding

Preparation Time: 10 minutes | **Cooking Time:** 0 minutes (overnight refrigeration) | **Serving Size:** 2

Ingredients:
- 1/2 cup chia seeds
- 2 cups almond milk
- 1 teaspoon vanilla extract
- 1 tablespoon maple syrup
- 1/2 cup mixed berries

Mode of cooking:
- Mixing and refrigeration

Procedure:
1. In a medium bowl, combine chia seeds, almond milk, vanilla extract, and maple syrup. Stir well.
2. Cover the bowl and refrigerate overnight or for at least 4 hours until the mixture thickens.
3. Stir the chia pudding and divide into two bowls.
4. Top each bowl with mixed berries.
5. Serve chilled.

Nutrition (Per serving): Calories: 220 | Fat: 10g | Carbs: 28g | Protein: 6g | Sugar: 10g | Sodium: 40mg

76.   Nut and Fruit Energy Bites

Preparation Time: 15 minutes | **Cooking Time:** 0 minutes | **Serving Size:** 2

Ingredients:
- 1 cup rolled oats
- 1/2 cup almond butter
- 1/4 cup honey
- 1/4 cup dried cranberries
- 1/4 cup chopped nuts (almonds, walnuts)
- 1 tablespoon chia seeds

Mode of cooking:
- Mixing and chilling

Procedure:
1. In a large bowl, combine rolled oats, almond butter, honey, dried cranberries, chopped nuts, and chia seeds.
2. Mix well until all ingredients are thoroughly combined.
3. Roll the mixture into small balls using your hands.
4. Place the energy bites on a plate and refrigerate for at least 1 hour.
5. Serve chilled or at room temperature.

Nutrition (Per serving): Calories: 250 | Fat: 14g | Carbs: 28g | Protein: 6g | Sugar: 15g | Sodium: 60mg

77. Berry Smoothie

Preparation Time: 10 minutes | **Cooking Time:** 0 minutes | **Serving Size:** 2

Ingredients:
- 1 cup mixed berries (strawberries, blueberries, raspberries)
- 1 banana
- 1 cup almond milk
- 1 tablespoon flax seeds
- 1 teaspoon honey (optional)

Mode of cooking:
- Blending

Procedure:
1. Wash and prepare the mixed berries.
2. Peel and slice the banana.
3. In a blender, combine berries, banana, almond milk, flax seeds, and honey if using.
4. Blend until smooth.
5. Pour into glasses and serve immediately.

Nutrition (Per serving): Calories: 180 | Fat: 4g | Carbs: 36g | Protein: 4g | Sugar: 20g | Sodium: 40mg

78. Cucumber and Avocado Salad

Preparation Time: 10 minutes | **Cooking Time:** 0 minutes | **Serving Size:** 2

Ingredients:
- 1 cucumber, diced
- 1 avocado, diced
- 1 tablespoon lemon juice
- 1 tablespoon olive oil
- Salt and pepper to taste

Mode of cooking:
- Assembling

Procedure:
1. Dice the cucumber and avocado.
2. In a bowl, combine the diced cucumber and avocado.
3. Drizzle with lemon juice and olive oil.
4. Season with salt and pepper.
5. Toss gently to combine and serve immediately.

Nutrition (Per serving): Calories: 180 | Fat: 14g | Carbs: 12g | Protein: 2g | Sugar: 2g | Sodium: 10mg

79. Roasted Chickpeas

Preparation Time: 10 minutes | **Cooking Time:** 30 minutes | **Serving Size:** 2

Ingredients:
- 1 can chickpeas, drained and rinsed
- 1 tablespoon olive oil
- 1 teaspoon paprika
- 1/2 teaspoon garlic powder
- Salt and pepper to taste

Mode of cooking:
- Baking

Procedure:
1. Preheat the oven to 400°F (200°C).
2. In a bowl, toss the chickpeas with olive oil, paprika, garlic powder, salt, and pepper.
3. Spread the chickpeas on a baking sheet in a single layer.
4. Bake for 30 minutes, stirring halfway through, until crispy.
5. Let cool slightly before serving.

Nutrition (Per serving): Calories: 200 | Fat: 8g | Carbs: 24g | Protein: 8g | Sugar: 2g | Sodium: 300mg

80.   Caprese Skewers

Preparation Time: 10 minutes | **Cooking Time:** 0 minutes | **Serving Size:** 2

Ingredients:

- 10 cherry tomatoes
- 10 fresh mozzarella balls
- 10 fresh basil leaves
- 1 tablespoon balsamic glaze

Mode of cooking:

- Assembling

Procedure:

1. Thread a cherry tomato, a mozzarella ball, and a basil leaf onto each skewer.
2. Repeat until all ingredients are used.
3. Arrange the skewers on a plate.
4. Drizzle with balsamic glaze.
5. Serve immediately.

Nutrition (Per serving): Calories: 160 | Fat: 10g | Carbs: 6g | Protein: 10g | Sugar: 4g | Sodium: 200mg

81.   Mixed Nuts and Seeds

Preparation Time: 5 minutes | **Cooking Time:** 0 minutes | **Serving Size:** 2

Ingredients:

- 1/4 cup almonds
- 1/4 cup walnuts
- 1/4 cup pumpkin seeds
- 1/4 cup sunflower seeds

Mode of cooking:

- Assembling

Procedure:

1. In a bowl, combine almonds, walnuts, pumpkin seeds, and sunflower seeds.
2. Mix well to combine.
3. Divide into small containers or bags for easy snacking.

4. Serve immediately or store for later use.

Nutrition (Per serving): Calories: 240 | Fat: 20g | Carbs: 10g | Protein: 8g | Sugar: 2g | Sodium: 5mg

82.　Edamame

Preparation Time: 5 minutes | **Cooking Time:** 5 minutes | **Serving Size:** 2

Ingredients:
- 1 cup edamame (in pods)
- 1 tablespoon sea salt

Mode of cooking:
- Boiling

Procedure:
1. Bring a pot of water to a boil.
2. Add the edamame pods and boil for 5 minutes until tender.
3. Drain the edamame and sprinkle with sea salt.
4. Serve warm or chilled.

Nutrition (Per serving): Calories: 140 | Fat: 4g | Carbs: 12g | Protein: 12g | Sugar: 2g | Sodium: 400mg

83.　Avocado Deviled Eggs

Preparation Time: 10 minutes | **Cooking Time:** 10 minutes | **Serving Size:** 2

Ingredients:
- 4 eggs
- 1 avocado
- 1 tablespoon lime juice
- Salt and pepper to taste
- Paprika for garnish

Mode of cooking:
- Boiling and assembling

Procedure:
1. Place the eggs in a pot and cover with water. Bring to a boil and cook for 10 minutes.
2. Remove the eggs from the boiling water and place them in an ice bath. Once cool, peel the eggs.
3. Cut the eggs in half and remove the yolks. Place the yolks in a bowl.
4. Mash the avocado with the egg yolks and lime juice. Season with salt and pepper.
5. Spoon the avocado mixture back into the egg whites. Sprinkle with paprika and serve.

Nutrition (Per serving): Calories: 180 | Fat: 14g | Carbs: 6g | Protein: 10g | Sugar: 1g | Sodium: 200mg

84. Cucumber Hummus Boats

Preparation Time: 10 minutes | **Cooking Time:** 0 minutes | **Serving Size:** 2

Ingredients:
- 1 cucumber
- 1/2 cup hummus
- 1 tablespoon fresh dill, chopped
- 1 teaspoon lemon zest

Mode of cooking:
- Assembling

Procedure:
1. Slice the cucumber lengthwise and scoop out the seeds to create a boat shape.
2. Fill each cucumber boat with hummus.
3. Sprinkle fresh dill and lemon zest over the hummus.
4. Serve immediately.

Nutrition (Per serving): Calories: 110 | Fat: 5g | Carbs: 12g | Protein: 4g | Sugar: 3g | Sodium: 250mg

85. Almond Flour Crackers with Guacamole

Preparation Time: 10 minutes | **Cooking Time:** 15 minutes | **Serving Size:** 2

Ingredients:
- 1 cup almond flour
- 1 egg
- 1/2 teaspoon salt
- 1 avocado
- 1 tablespoon lime juice
- 1/4 teaspoon garlic powder
- Salt and pepper to taste

Mode of cooking:
- Baking and assembling

Procedure:
1. Preheat the oven to 350°F (175°C).
2. In a bowl, mix almond flour, egg, and salt until a dough forms.
3. Roll out the dough between two sheets of parchment paper and cut into cracker shapes.
4. Place the crackers on a baking sheet and bake for 15 minutes until golden brown.
5. In a separate bowl, mash the avocado with lime juice, garlic powder, salt, and pepper. Serve the crackers with guacamole.

Nutrition (Per serving): Calories: 250 | Fat: 20g | Carbs: 10g | Protein: 8g | Sugar: 1g | Sodium: 300mg

86. Apple Nachos

Preparation Time: 10 minutes | **Cooking Time:** 0 minutes | **Serving Size:** 2

Ingredients:
- 1 large apple, sliced
- 2 tablespoons almond butter
- 1 tablespoon shredded coconut
- 1 tablespoon dark chocolate chips
- 1 teaspoon chia seeds

Mode of cooking:

- Assembling

Procedure:
1. Wash and slice the apple into thin rounds.
2. Arrange the apple slices on a plate.
3. Drizzle almond butter over the apple slices.
4. Sprinkle shredded coconut, dark chocolate chips, and chia seeds on top.
5. Serve immediately.

Nutrition (Per serving): Calories: 200 | Fat: 12g | Carbs: 24g | Protein: 3g | Sugar: 18g | Sodium: 5mg

87. Tropical Smoothie Bowl

Preparation Time: 10 minutes | **Cooking Time:** 0 minutes | **Serving Size:** 2

Ingredients:
- 1 cup frozen mango chunks
- 1 cup frozen pineapple chunks
- 1 banana
- 1 cup coconut milk
- 1/4 cup granola
- 2 tablespoons shredded coconut
- 1 tablespoon chia seeds

Mode of cooking:
- Blending and assembling

Procedure:
1. In a blender, combine frozen mango, frozen pineapple, banana, and coconut milk. Blend until smooth.
2. Divide the smoothie mixture between two bowls.
3. Top each bowl with granola, shredded coconut, and chia seeds.
4. Serve immediately with a spoon.

Nutrition (Per serving): Calories: 250 | Fat: 12g | Carbs: 36g | Protein: 3g | Sugar: 24g | Sodium: 30mg

Anti-inflammatory Desserts

88.   Turmeric Mango Sorbet

Preparation Time: 10 minutes | **Cooking Time:** 0 minutes (Freezing time: 4 hours) | **Serving Size:** 2

Ingredients:
- 2 cups frozen mango chunks
- 1/2 cup coconut milk
- 1 teaspoon turmeric powder
- 1 tablespoon honey
- 1 teaspoon lime juice

Mode of cooking:
- Blending and freezing

Procedure:
1. In a blender, combine frozen mango chunks, coconut milk, turmeric powder, honey, and lime juice.
2. Blend until smooth and creamy.
3. Transfer the mixture to a shallow container.
4. Freeze for at least 4 hours, stirring every hour to ensure an even texture.
5. Scoop into bowls and serve immediately.

Nutrition (Per serving): Calories: 150 | Fat: 5g | Carbs: 30g | Protein: 1g | Sugar: 24g | Sodium: 10mg

89. Blueberry Chia Pudding

Preparation Time: 10 minutes | **Cooking Time:** 0 minutes (Refrigeration time: 4 hours) | **Serving Size:** 2

Ingredients:
- 1/2 cup chia seeds
- 2 cups almond milk
- 1 teaspoon vanilla extract
- 1 tablespoon maple syrup
- 1 cup fresh blueberries

Mode of cooking:
- Mixing and refrigeration

Procedure:
1. In a medium bowl, combine chia seeds, almond milk, vanilla extract, and maple syrup. Stir well.
2. Cover the bowl and refrigerate for at least 4 hours or overnight until the mixture thickens.
3. Stir the chia pudding and divide into two bowls.
4. Top each bowl with fresh blueberries.
5. Serve chilled.

Nutrition (Per serving): Calories: 220 | Fat: 10g | Carbs: 28g | Protein: 6g | Sugar: 10g | Sodium: 40mg

90. Avocado Chocolate Mousse

Preparation Time: 10 minutes | **Cooking Time:** 0 minutes | **Serving Size:** 2

Ingredients:
- 2 ripe avocados
- 1/4 cup cocoa powder
- 1/4 cup honey
- 1 teaspoon vanilla extract
- 1/4 cup almond milk

Mode of cooking:
- Blending

Procedure:
1. Scoop the flesh of the avocados into a blender.
2. Add cocoa powder, honey, vanilla extract, and almond milk.
3. Blend until smooth and creamy.
4. Divide the mousse into two bowls.
5. Serve immediately or chill in the refrigerator before serving.

Nutrition (Per serving): Calories: 320 | Fat: 20g | Carbs: 34g | Protein: 3g | Sugar: 20g | Sodium: 20mg

91. Apple Cinnamon Bites

Preparation Time: 10 minutes | **Cooking Time:** 0 minutes | **Serving Size:** 2

Ingredients:
- 1 large apple, chopped
- 1/2 cup rolled oats
- 1/4 cup almond butter
- 1 tablespoon honey
- 1 teaspoon cinnamon
- 1 teaspoon chia seeds

Mode of cooking:
- Assembling

Procedure:
1. In a medium bowl, combine chopped apple, rolled oats, almond butter, honey, cinnamon, and chia seeds.
2. Mix well until all ingredients are thoroughly combined.
3. Roll the mixture into small balls using your hands.
4. Place the apple cinnamon bites on a plate and refrigerate for at least 30 minutes.
5. Serve chilled.

Nutrition (Per serving): Calories: 180 | Fat: 10g | Carbs: 20g | Protein: 4g | Sugar: 12g | Sodium: 10mg

92. Pineapple Coconut Bars

Preparation Time: 15 minutes | **Cooking Time:** 0 minutes (Freezing time: 1 hour) | **Serving Size:** 2

Ingredients:
- 1 cup pineapple chunks
- 1/2 cup shredded coconut
- 1/4 cup coconut oil, melted
- 1 tablespoon honey
- 1 teaspoon lime zest

Mode of cooking:
- Blending and freezing

Procedure:
1. In a blender, combine pineapple chunks, shredded coconut, melted coconut oil, honey, and lime zest.
2. Blend until smooth.
3. Pour the mixture into a shallow container lined with parchment paper.
4. Freeze for at least 1 hour until firm.
5. Cut into bars and serve immediately.

Nutrition (Per serving): Calories: 200 | Fat: 14g | Carbs: 20g | Protein: 2g | Sugar: 14g | Sodium: 5mg

93. Berry Almond Crumble

Preparation Time: 10 minutes | **Cooking Time:** 20 minutes | **Serving Size:** 2

Ingredients:
- 1 cup mixed berries (strawberries, blueberries, raspberries)
- 1/4 cup almond flour
- 2 tablespoons rolled oats
- 2 tablespoons almond butter
- 1 tablespoon honey
- 1 teaspoon cinnamon

Mode of cooking:

- Baking

Procedure:
1. Preheat the oven to 350°F (175°C).
2. In a small baking dish, layer the mixed berries.
3. In a bowl, combine almond flour, rolled oats, almond butter, honey, and cinnamon. Mix until crumbly.
4. Sprinkle the crumble mixture over the berries.
5. Bake for 20 minutes until the top is golden brown. Serve warm.

Nutrition (Per serving): Calories: 220 | Fat: 14g | Carbs: 22g | Protein: 4g | Sugar: 14g | Sodium: 20mg

94. Banana Oat Cookies

Preparation Time: 10 minutes | **Cooking Time:** 15 minutes | **Serving Size:** 2

Ingredients:
- 2 ripe bananas, mashed
- 1 cup rolled oats
- 1/4 cup almond butter
- 1/4 cup dark chocolate chips
- 1 teaspoon vanilla extract

Mode of cooking:
- Baking

Procedure:
1. Preheat the oven to 350°F (175°C).
2. In a bowl, combine mashed bananas, rolled oats, almond butter, dark chocolate chips, and vanilla extract.
3. Mix well until all ingredients are thoroughly combined.
4. Drop spoonfuls of the mixture onto a baking sheet lined with parchment paper.
5. Bake for 15 minutes until the edges are golden brown. Let cool before serving.

Nutrition (Per serving): Calories: 180 | Fat: 10g | Carbs: 24g | Protein: 4g | Sugar: 8g | Sodium: 30mg

95. Coconut Mango Chia Pudding

Preparation Time: 10 minutes | **Cooking Time:** 0 minutes (Refrigeration time: 4 hours) | **Serving Size:** 2

Ingredients:

- 1/2 cup chia seeds
- 2 cups coconut milk
- 1 tablespoon honey
- 1 teaspoon vanilla extract
- 1 cup diced mango

Mode of cooking:

- Mixing and refrigeration

Procedure:

1. In a medium bowl, combine chia seeds, coconut milk, honey, and vanilla extract. Stir well.
2. Cover the bowl and refrigerate for at least 4 hours or overnight until the mixture thickens.
3. Stir the chia pudding and divide into two bowls.
4. Top each bowl with diced mango.
5. Serve chilled.

Nutrition (Per serving): Calories: 250 | Fat: 14g | Carbs: 30g | Protein: 6g | Sugar: 18g | Sodium: 20mg

96. Almond Joy Bites

Preparation Time: 15 minutes | **Cooking Time:** 0 minutes (Refrigeration time: 1 hour) | **Serving Size:** 2

Ingredients:

- 1 cup shredded coconut
- 1/4 cup coconut oil, melted
- 1/4 cup almond butter
- 2 tablespoons honey
- 1/4 cup dark chocolate chips

Mode of cooking:

- Mixing and refrigeration

Procedure:
1. In a bowl, combine shredded coconut, melted coconut oil, almond butter, and honey. Mix well.
2. Roll the mixture into small balls.
3. Place the balls on a plate and refrigerate for at least 1 hour until firm.
4. Melt the dark chocolate chips in a microwave-safe bowl.
5. Drizzle the melted chocolate over the chilled coconut balls and serve.

Nutrition (Per serving): Calories: 280 | Fat: 20g | Carbs: 24g | Protein: 4g | Sugar: 16g | Sodium: 10mg

97. Turmeric Ginger Smoothie

Preparation Time: 10 minutes | **Cooking Time:** 0 minutes | **Serving Size:** 2

Ingredients:
- 1 banana
- 1 cup almond milk
- 1/2 teaspoon turmeric powder
- 1/2 teaspoon ginger powder
- 1 tablespoon honey
- 1/2 cup ice cubes

Mode of cooking:
- Blending

Procedure:
1. Peel and slice the banana.
2. In a blender, combine banana, almond milk, turmeric powder, ginger powder, honey, and ice cubes.
3. Blend until smooth.
4. Pour into glasses and serve immediately.

Nutrition (Per serving): Calories: 140 | Fat: 2g | Carbs: 30g | Protein: 2g | Sugar: 20g | Sodium: 60mg

98. Matcha Green Tea Energy Bites

Preparation Time: 15 minutes | **Cooking Time:** 0 minutes (Refrigeration time: 1 hour) | **Serving Size:** 2

Ingredients:

- 1 cup rolled oats
- 1/4 cup almond butter
- 1/4 cup honey
- 1 tablespoon matcha green tea powder
- 1 tablespoon chia seeds

Mode of cooking:

- Mixing and refrigeration

Procedure:

1. In a large bowl, combine rolled oats, almond butter, honey, matcha green tea powder, and chia seeds.
2. Mix well until all ingredients are thoroughly combined.
3. Roll the mixture into small balls using your hands.
4. Place the energy bites on a plate and refrigerate for at least 1 hour.
5. Serve chilled or at room temperature.

Nutrition (Per serving): Calories: 180 | Fat: 10g | Carbs: 22g | Protein: 4g | Sugar: 12g | Sodium: 20mg

99. Dark Chocolate Avocado Truffles

Preparation Time: 15 minutes | **Cooking Time:** 0 minutes (Refrigeration time: 1 hour) | **Serving Size:** 2

Ingredients:

- 1 ripe avocado
- 1/4 cup cocoa powder
- 1/4 cup dark chocolate chips, melted
- 1 tablespoon honey
- 1 teaspoon vanilla extract

Mode of cooking:

- Blending and refrigeration

Procedure:
1. Scoop the flesh of the avocado into a blender.
2. Add cocoa powder, melted dark chocolate, honey, and vanilla extract.
3. Blend until smooth and creamy.
4. Roll the mixture into small balls.
5. Place the truffles on a plate and refrigerate for at least 1 hour before serving.

Nutrition (Per serving): Calories: 220 | Fat: 14g | Carbs: 20g | Protein: 2g | Sugar: 12g | Sodium: 10mg

100. Coconut Matcha Latte

Preparation Time: 5 minutes | **Cooking Time:** 5 minutes | **Serving Size:** 2

Ingredients:
- 2 cups coconut milk
- 1 teaspoon matcha green tea powder
- 1 tablespoon honey
- 1/2 teaspoon vanilla extract

Mode of cooking:
- Simmering and blending

Procedure:
1. In a small saucepan, heat the coconut milk over medium heat until warm.
2. In a small bowl, whisk together matcha green tea powder and honey.
3. Add the matcha mixture to the warm coconut milk and stir to combine.
4. Remove from heat and stir in vanilla extract.
5. Pour into mugs and serve immediately.

Nutrition (Per serving): Calories: 120 | Fat: 8g | Carbs: 12g | Protein: 1g | Sugar: 10g | Sodium: 5mg

101. Baked Pears with Walnuts and Honey

Preparation Time: 10 minutes | **Cooking Time:** 25 minutes | **Serving Size:** 2

Ingredients:

- 2 pears, halved and cored
- 1/4 cup walnuts, chopped
- 2 tablespoons honey
- 1 teaspoon cinnamon

Mode of cooking:

- Baking

Procedure:

1. Preheat the oven to 350°F (175°C).
2. Place the pear halves in a baking dish.
3. In a small bowl, combine chopped walnuts, honey, and cinnamon.
4. Spoon the walnut mixture into the center of each pear half.
5. Bake for 25 minutes until the pears are tender. Serve warm.

Nutrition (Per serving): Calories: 180 | Fat: 8g | Carbs: 28g | Protein: 2g | Sugar: 20g | Sodium: 5mg

102. Chocolate Banana Ice Cream

Preparation Time: 10 minutes | **Cooking Time:** 0 minutes (Freezing time: 4 hours) | **Serving Size:** 2

Ingredients:

- 2 ripe bananas, sliced and frozen
- 2 tablespoons cocoa powder
- 1 tablespoon almond butter
- 1 teaspoon vanilla extract

Mode of cooking:

- Blending and freezing

Procedure:
1. Place the frozen banana slices in a blender.
2. Add cocoa powder, almond butter, and vanilla extract.
3. Blend until smooth and creamy.
4. Transfer the mixture to a shallow container.
5. Freeze for at least 4 hours before serving.

Nutrition (Per serving): Calories: 160 | Fat: 6g | Carbs: 28g | Protein: 2g | Sugar: 18g | Sodium: 10mg

103. Mango Coconut Chia Popsicles

Preparation Time: 15 minutes | **Cooking Time:** 0 minutes (Freezing time: 4 hours) | **Serving Size:** 2

Ingredients:
- 1 cup diced mango
- 1 cup coconut milk
- 1/4 cup chia seeds
- 1 tablespoon honey

Mode of cooking:
- Blending and freezing

Procedure:
1. In a blender, combine diced mango, coconut milk, chia seeds, and honey.
2. Blend until smooth.
3. Pour the mixture into popsicle molds.
4. Freeze for at least 4 hours until solid.
5. Remove from molds and serve.

Nutrition (Per serving): Calories: 140 | Fat: 8g | Carbs: 18g | Protein: 2g | Sugar: 12g | Sodium: 5mg

104. Lemon Coconut Balls

Preparation Time: 10 minutes | **Cooking Time:** 0 minutes (Refrigeration time: 1 hour) | **Serving Size:** 2

Ingredients:
- 1 cup shredded coconut
- 2 tablespoons coconut oil, melted
- 2 tablespoons honey
- 1 tablespoon lemon zest
- 1 tablespoon lemon juice

Mode of cooking:
- Mixing and refrigeration

Procedure:
1. In a bowl, combine shredded coconut, melted coconut oil, honey, lemon zest, and lemon juice.
2. Mix well until all ingredients are thoroughly combined.
3. Roll the mixture into small balls.
4. Place the balls on a plate and refrigerate for at least 1 hour until firm.
5. Serve chilled.

Nutrition (Per serving): Calories: 180 | Fat: 14g | Carbs: 16g | Protein: 2g | Sugar: 12g | Sodium: 5mg

105. Raspberry Almond Bars

Preparation Time: 15 minutes | **Cooking Time:** 20 minutes | **Serving Size:** 2

Ingredients:
- 1 cup almond flour
- 1/4 cup coconut oil, melted
- 1/4 cup honey
- 1/2 cup fresh raspberries
- 1 tablespoon chia seeds

Mode of cooking:
- Baking

Procedure:
1. Preheat the oven to 350°F (175°C).
2. In a bowl, mix almond flour, melted coconut oil, and honey until a dough forms.
3. Press the dough into the bottom of a small baking dish.
4. In another bowl, mash the raspberries and stir in chia seeds.
5. Spread the raspberry mixture over the almond crust.
6. Bake for 20 minutes until the top is set. Let cool before cutting into bars and serving.

Nutrition (Per serving): Calories: 220 | Fat: 16g | Carbs: 20g | Protein: 4g | Sugar: 14g | Sodium: 5mg

Chapter 7: 28-Day Meal Plan

Day	Breakfast	Snack 1	Lunch	Dinner
1	Green Power Smoothie	Apple and Almond Butter Bites	Quinoa and Kale Salad	Baked Lemon Herb Salmon
2	Berry Bliss Smoothie	Greek Yogurt Parfait	Chickpea and Spinach Salad	Quinoa Stuffed Bell Peppers
3	Tropical Delight Smoothie	Avocado Toast	Avocado and Tomato Salad	Zucchini Noodles with Pesto
4	Almond Berry Smoothie	Veggie Sticks with Hummus	Mediterranean Cucumber Salad	Baked Cod with Asparagus
5	Matcha Green Tea Smoothie	Chia Pudding	Beet and Walnut Salad	Chickpea and Spinach Curry
6	Chocolate Banana Smoothie	Nut and Fruit Energy Bites	Apple and Pecan Salad	Lemon Herb Chicken and Vegetables
7	Pumpkin Spice Smoothie	Berry Smoothie	Lentil and Arugula Salad	Spaghetti Squash with Tomato Basil Sauce
8	Blueberry Oat Smoothie	Cucumber and Avocado Salad	Strawberry and Spinach Salad	Mediterranean Chickpea Salad
9	Avocado Pineapple Smoothie	Greek Yogurt Parfait	Mango and Avocado Salad	Baked Eggplant Parmesan
10	Spinach Pear Smoothie	Apple and Almond Butter Bites	Broccoli and Quinoa Salad	Lemon Garlic Shrimp and Zoodles
11	Quinoa Fruit Bowl	Edamame	Sweet Potato and Lentil Soup	Grilled Chicken with Mango Salsa
12	Almond Joy Smoothie Bowl	Veggie Sticks with Hummus	Carrot Ginger Soup	Stuffed Portobello Mushrooms

13	Chia Pudding Bowl	Nut and Fruit Energy Bites	Chickpea and Spinach Stew	Baked Tilapia with Lemon and Dill
14	Tropical Overnight Oats	Berry Smoothie	Butternut Squash and Apple Soup	Vegan Lentil Shepherd's Pie
15	Savory Avocado Quinoa Bowl	Greek Yogurt Parfait	Red Lentil and Tomato Stew	Roasted Vegetable and Chickpea Bowl
16	Blueberry Almond Breakfast Bowl	Veggie Sticks with Hummus	Green Pea and Mint Soup	Baked Garlic Butter Shrimp
17	Apple Cinnamon Breakfast Bowl	Edamame	Turmeric Cauliflower Soup	Herb-Crusted Salmon
18	Banana Nut Breakfast Bowl	Avocado Toast	Sweet Potato and Black Bean Stew	Lemon Herb Tilapia
19	Tropical Chia Bowl	Mixed Nuts and Seeds	Broccoli and White Bean Soup	Baked Cod with Tomato Basil Sauce
20	Sweet Potato Breakfast Bowl	Apple and Almond Butter Bites	Zucchini and Basil Soup	Garlic Lemon Shrimp Skewers
21	Green Power Smoothie	Nut and Fruit Energy Bites	Quinoa and Kale Salad	Baked Scallops with Lemon Butter
22	Berry Bliss Smoothie	Veggie Sticks with Hummus	Chickpea and Spinach Salad	Baked Halibut with Pesto
23	Tropical Delight Smoothie	Apple and Almond Butter Bites	Avocado and Tomato Salad	Citrus Herb Grilled Salmon
24	Almond Berry Smoothie	Greek Yogurt Parfait	Mediterranean Cucumber Salad	Baked Trout with Dill
25	Matcha Green Tea Smoothie	Edamame	Beet and Walnut Salad	Lemon Herb Baked Haddock
26	Chocolate Banana Smoothie	Nut and Fruit Energy Bites	Apple and Pecan Salad	Garlic Butter Baked Lobster Tail

27	Pumpkin Spice Smoothie	Berry Smoothie	Lentil and Arugula Salad	Baked Swordfish with Capers and Olives
28	Blueberry Oat Smoothie	Cucumber and Avocado Salad	Strawberry and Spinach Salad	Honey Lime Baked Mahi Mahi

Shopping List

Produce
- Apples (10)
- Avocados (14)
- Bananas (10)
- Beet (2)
- Bell peppers (4)
- Blueberries (4 cups)
- Broccoli (4 heads)
- Carrots (8)
- Cherry tomatoes (4 cups)
- Chickpeas (canned, 8 cups)
- Cucumbers (8)
- Fresh herbs (dill, parsley, cilantro, basil)
- Garlic (2 bulbs)
- Ginger (2 knobs)
- Grapes (for snacks, optional)
- Kale (4 bunches)
- Kiwifruit (4)
- Lemons (10)
- Limes (10)
- Mangoes (6)
- Mixed berries (10 cups)
- Mushrooms (portobello, 4)
- Oranges (4)
- Pears (6)
- Pineapple (4 cups)
- Quinoa (dry, 4 cups)
- Red onion (6)
- Spinach (12 bunches)
- Strawberries (8 cups)
- Sweet potatoes (12)
- Zucchini (10)

Proteins
- Chicken breasts (4)
- Cod fillets (4)
- Eggs (dozen)
- Halibut (4 fillets)
- Salmon (6 fillets)
- Scallops (4)
- Shrimp (2 lbs)
- Tilapia (4 fillets)
- Trout (4 fillets)

Dairy & Alternatives
- Almond butter (2 jars)
- Almond milk (4 cartons)
- Coconut milk (8 cans)
- Greek yogurt (4 tubs)
- Mozzarella balls (8 oz)
- Parmesan cheese (4 oz)
- Pesto (1 jar)

Dry Goods
- Almond flour (4 cups)
- Almonds (2 cups)
- Chia seeds (2 cups)
- Cocoa powder (1 cup)
- Coconut flakes (1 cup)
- Dark chocolate chips (2 cups)
- Flax seeds (1 cup)
- Honey (1 jar)
- Maple syrup (1 bottle)
- Nut butter (1 jar)

- Oats (8 cups)
- Pumpkin seeds (1 cup)
- Quinoa (4 cups)
- Rice vinegar (1 bottle)
- Rolled oats (8 cups)
- Sesame seeds (1 cup)
- Soy sauce (1 bottle)
- Sunflower seeds (1 cup)
- Walnuts (1 cup)

Spices & Seasonings
- Black pepper
- Cinnamon
- Cumin
- Garlic powder
- Ginger powder
- Matcha green tea powder
- Oregano
- Paprika
- Red pepper flakes
- Sea salt
- Turmeric powder
- Vanilla extract

Condiments & Oils
- Apple cider vinegar (1 bottle)
- Balsamic glaze (1 bottle)
- Coconut oil (1 jar)
- Extra virgin olive oil (1 bottle)
- Red wine vinegar (1 bottle)

Snacks
- Almond flour crackers (store-bought or homemade)
- Hummus (store-bought or homemade)
- Mixed nuts (2 cups)
- Nut and fruit energy bites (store-bought or homemade)
- Veggie sticks (cucumbers, carrots, bell peppers)

Freezer
- Frozen blueberries (4 cups)
- Frozen mango chunks (6 cups)
- Frozen pineapple chunks (4 cups)

Chapter 9: Frequently Asked Questions

Myths and Facts about the Anti-inflammatory Diet

The concept of an anti-inflammatory diet has garnered substantial attention, but with its rise in popularity, numerous misconceptions have emerged. It is essential to dispel these myths to fully appreciate the benefits of this eating approach.

One widespread myth is that this diet is inherently restrictive and devoid of pleasure. Many people mistakenly believe that adopting such a dietary regimen means bidding farewell to tasty foods and resigning oneself to bland, uninspiring meals. In reality, the opposite is true. This eating plan emphasizes a variety of colorful fruits and vegetables, whole grains, lean proteins, and healthy fats. This approach not only offers a spectrum of flavors and textures but also ensures that meals are both enjoyable and satisfying. From succulent herb-crusted salmon to refreshing berry smoothies, the options are plentiful and diverse.

Another common misconception is that this dietary regimen is a short-term fix rather than a sustainable lifestyle change. Some individuals view it as a temporary solution to combat inflammation, akin to a crash diet aimed at quick results. However, this way of eating is designed for long-term commitment to health. It's about consistently choosing foods that reduce inflammation and promote overall well-being. By integrating these principles into daily routines, one can maintain lower inflammation levels and enjoy the associated health benefits over the long haul.

A third myth suggests that only people with chronic illnesses or inflammatory conditions can benefit from this diet. While it is true that those with conditions like arthritis or inflammatory bowel disease may see significant improvements, the benefits extend to everyone. Chronic inflammation is linked to numerous health issues, including heart disease, diabetes, and even certain cancers. By following this eating plan, anyone can enhance their overall health, improve immune function, and potentially prevent various diseases.

There is also a belief that such a diet is complicated and difficult to follow. This misconception often arises from the idea that one must source exotic ingredients or prepare elaborate meals. In fact, the foundation of this regimen lies in simplicity. Fresh, whole foods are the cornerstone, and many recipes are straightforward and quick to prepare. For instance, a simple quinoa salad with fresh vegetables and a light vinaigrette can be made in minutes and offers a wholesome, anti-inflammatory meal option.

Lastly, some people think that this diet means eliminating all fats. This myth couldn't be further from the truth. Healthy fats, such as those found in olive oil, avocados, nuts, and fatty fish, are essential components. These fats help reduce inflammation and support heart health. It's the trans fats and excessive saturated fats that should be minimized, as they can contribute to inflammation.

Common Mistakes and How to Avoid Them

One frequent error is the assumption that all fats are detrimental. While it's true that trans fats and excessive saturated fats can promote inflammation, healthy fats are a vital part of this dietary approach. Sources like olive oil, avocados, nuts, and fatty fish are rich in omega-3 fatty acids, which actually help reduce inflammation. Avoid the trap of eliminating fats altogether. Instead, focus on incorporating beneficial fats into your meals.

Another common misstep is relying heavily on processed foods labeled as "healthy" or "anti-inflammatory." Many packaged products boast health claims but are often laden with hidden sugars, unhealthy oils, and preservatives that can trigger inflammation. Whole foods, in their natural state, should be the cornerstone of your diet. Fresh fruits, vegetables, lean proteins, and whole grains are far more beneficial than any processed alternatives.

Failing to diversify your food choices is another common mistake. Eating the same foods repeatedly can lead to nutrient deficiencies and make meals monotonous. Variety is essential not only for getting a range of nutrients but also for keeping your meals interesting and satisfying. Experiment with different fruits, vegetables, grains, and proteins to ensure a well-rounded intake of essential nutrients.

A lack of proper meal planning can also hinder your progress. Without planning, you might find yourself reaching for convenience foods that do not align with your dietary goals. Dedicate time each week to plan your meals and snacks, making sure you have all necessary ingredients on hand. This preparation can prevent impulsive eating and help you stay on track.

Overlooking the importance of hydration is a mistake many make. Staying well-hydrated is vital for maintaining overall health and aiding in the reduction of inflammation. Water is the best choice, but herbal teas and infused waters are also good options. Be cautious with sugary drinks and sodas, which can contribute to inflammation and counteract your efforts.

Another pitfall is not listening to your body. An anti-inflammatory diet is not a one-size-fits-all solution. Pay attention to how different foods make you feel. Some foods that are generally considered anti-inflammatory might not agree with everyone. It's important to adjust your diet based on your body's responses and needs.

Lastly, many people forget the importance of balance. While focusing on reducing inflammation is crucial, it's also essential to enjoy your meals and maintain a positive relationship with food. Deprivation and over-restriction can lead to unhealthy eating patterns and make it harder to sustain this way of eating. Allow yourself to indulge occasionally and enjoy the process of discovering new, delicious, and healthy foods.

Conclusion

As we reach the end of our journey through the principles and practices of an anti-inflammatory lifestyle, it's essential to reflect on the transformative potential of this approach. Embracing an anti-inflammatory diet is not just about the foods you eat; it's about cultivating a holistic lifestyle that promotes overall well-being, longevity, and vitality.

Throughout these pages, we have explored a wide array of delicious, nutritious recipes designed to reduce inflammation and support your body's natural healing processes. From vibrant smoothies and wholesome salads to satisfying soups and flavorful dinners, each meal has been crafted to provide essential nutrients, antioxidants, and healthy fats that work synergistically to combat inflammation.

Beyond the recipes, we've delved into the science behind inflammation and how it impacts our health. Understanding the root causes of inflammation empowers us to make informed choices that go beyond mere symptom management. By focusing on prevention through diet, we can address the underlying factors that contribute to chronic inflammation and its associated health issues.

It's also crucial to acknowledge the broader lifestyle factors that complement an anti-inflammatory diet. Regular physical activity, adequate sleep, stress management, and mindful eating are all integral components of a holistic approach to health. Together, these elements create a foundation for a balanced and fulfilling life.

As you move forward, remember that change doesn't happen overnight. Adopting a new way of eating and living is a gradual process, and it's important to be patient and kind to yourself. Celebrate your progress, no matter how small, and remain committed to your long-term health goals.

The path to reducing inflammation and enhancing your health is a journey worth embarking on. By nourishing your body with the right foods and making mindful lifestyle choices, you are investing in a future of improved wellness and vitality. May the knowledge and inspiration gained from this book guide you towards a healthier, happier, and more vibrant life.

Thank you for taking this journey with us, and here's to your health and well-being!

SCAN THE QR CODE

OR COPY AND TRY THE URL

https://qrco.de/bfM7hx

Printed in Great Britain
by Amazon